D1065451

Carnegie Public Library
Robinson, Illinois

William Blake

Also by James Daugherty

ANDY AND THE LION

DANIEL BOONE

POOR RICHARD

ABRAHAM LINCOLN

OF COURAGE UNDAUNTED

MARCUS AND NARCISSA WHITMAN, PIONEERS OF OREGON

WEST OF BOSTON

THE PICNIC

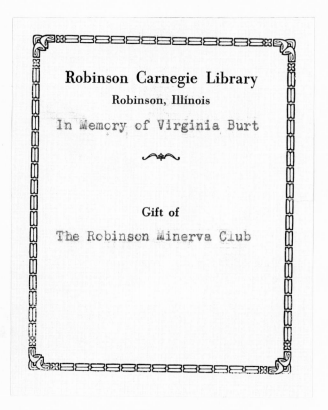

Robinson Carnegie Library

Robinson, Illinois

In Memory of Virginia Burt

Gift of

The Robinson Minerva Club

William Blake

BY JAMES DAUGHERTY

with reproductions of drawings
by William Blake

New York

THE VIKING PRESS

Carnegie Public Library
Robinson, Illinois

*This book
is affectionately dedicated
to my dear aunt Alice Telfair*

Copyright © 1960 by James Daugherty
All rights reserved
First published in 1960 by The Viking Press, Inc.
625 Madison Avenue, New York 22, N. Y.
Published simultaneously in Canada
by The Macmillan Company of Canada Limited

Library of Congress catalog card number: 60-14401

Printed in the U.S.A. by the Vail-Ballou Press, Inc.

Contents

Contents

Just Imagine

William Blake was an obscure craftsman, an engraver who lived all his outwardly uneventful life in London during the latter part of the eighteenth century and the early part of the nineteenth. He made barely enough money to keep himself and his devoted wife Catherine decently clothed and fed. And although he produced an enormous amount of work he never received recognition during his lifetime and was thought a complete artistic failure by many of his more successful contemporaries.

Not very interesting, you will say—that is, if that was all there was to it. But that was *not* all there was to it.

There was quite a bit more, for Blake happened to be a genius who wrote poetry and painted pictures. He made his poems into little books which he designed, engraved, and printed himself. Each page, when he had colored it, was a living and beautiful thing.

He painted a great many pictures too, in water color— many of them hardly larger than a postcard in size. "Inventions," he called them, because they were not copied from nature but were imaginative visions, revelations of truth as he saw it.

His best poems were very short, a few stanzas that shot right up to the stars, like the vertical take-off of a jet plane.

Emily Dickinson said, "If I feel physically as if the top of my head were taken off, I know that is poetry." And she should know. She wrote that kind herself. So did William Blake.

And his pictures?

Have you ever walked along a country road at night in utter darkness, with a storm coming up and distant thunder? All of a sudden—*zip*—a flash of lightning rips a jagged tear across the dark and for a blinding instant you see everything as distinct and sharp as day.

That is the way it is with Blake's pictures.

Blake saw with what he called "spiritual vision," and he painted what he saw. Being an artist, he used line and color and form to make his visions into harmonies that were vivid and precise and very beautiful. He said, "I look through the eye, not with it."

In the olden days there was nothing peculiar about spiritual vision or about seeing visions. The Biblical prophets all had it, and since then poets and spiritual thinkers and seers have seen truth and beauty and written great poems and painted visionary pictures. There have not been many of them, though.

Today it sometimes seems we are getting nowhere faster than ever before. But perhaps if you and I took time out once in a while to read great poetry and to look at the glorious pictures in the museums we too might have more of that sense of joy and beauty that is called "vision." Walt Whitman said, "I loaf and invite my soul."

Blake said that for him the world was all imagination— we might say, "ideas." Ideas, or imagination, can be useful —not only to great poets or painters but also to scientists, engineers, business managers, salesmen, mechanics, and congressmen as well. Thomas Edison, Albert Einstein, Henry Ford, and Wilbur and Orville Wright, to mention a very few, had imagination and used it; maybe not in the way that Blake or Isaiah or Shakespeare did, but you can use your imagination in a lot of different ways. With imagination, the sky is the limit. Or is it?

Soon, very soon, you, the young people who are now in the schools and colleges will take over the controls, will make the big decisions. You will be at the instrument panels, throwing the switches that control world destiny—for one world, with peace and justice for all, or for a world divided by wars and threatened by degradation and destruction.

This is where your imagination and vision come into the picture. Backed by courage and faith, these are powerful tools for world peace and justice—more powerful than nuclear bombs and ICBM, the dreadful ultimate weapon, to abolish war forever and to establish permanently a world of sanity and creative peace for all mankind.

Vision and faith say, "It can be done, and now!" Imagination and courage say, "We can and we will do it!"

This is why I think that Blake's life and work are important and significant for us today—more so than ever before. It was obviously a battle from first to last, and in the end a great victory for vision and imagination over dullness, doubt, and fear; of individuality and originality over timidity, conformity, and material limitations.

This is why his songs and pictures thrill us today with their mysterious beauty and power, their splendid affirmations, and their wild and vaulting rhythms.

His pictures are now in the great museums and libraries

of England and the United States, and they do not come up for sale very often, but several years ago a small water color, thirteen by fifteen inches in size, was bought at auction (the Graham Robertson Collection sale, Christie's, London, 1946) for $38,850 by the National Gallery of Scotland.

Perhaps after all, in the long pull, we should not consider that William Blake was altogether a total failure, even in what he called "this vegetative world."

—JAMES DAUGHERTY

Weston, Connecticut

PART ONE

A Tree Full of Angels

(1757-1792)

Vision or Imagination is a representation of what Eternally Exists, Really and Unchangeably.

CHAPTER I

Golden Square

The Angel that presided o'er my birth
Said, "Little creature, form'd of Joy & Mirth,
Go love without the help of any Thing on Earth."

Not far from the heart of London there was a quiet residential section known as Golden Square. Here, in the middle of the eighteenth century, at 28 Broad Street, lived a respectable tradesman and his wife, James and Catherine Blake. Of their five children, four were boys and one a girl. Their names were James, William, John, Robert, and Catherine.

Mr. Blake kept a fairly prosperous hosiery shop on the ground floor of the house in which they lived. He was no different from the ordinary English Bible-reading Protestant, except that he studied the writings of the mystic philosopher Emanuel Swedenborg. He had heard the great preachers John Wesley and George Whitefield speak, and had been moved to think deeply about religion. So, faith in God, the visions of Swedenborg, and a deep interest in the Bible were a vital and normal part of education, reading, and discussion in the home life of the Blake family.

William, born in 1757, was the next-to-oldest boy, and the most intelligent of the children. His father recognized in the bright mind of the youth something that was different, that was inspired, that might be genius, and he understood and encouraged William to follow his impulses. Little William Blake learned to read and write at his mother's knee. He listened to the music of the Psalms and the noble rhythms of the English Bible read aloud with understanding. He wondered at the strange visions of Swedenborg, who his father believed was a prophet who saw beyond the sight of ordinary men. As the boy listened, shining images came and went in colored light before his eyes and word-music sang in his ears.

As he grew, he began to read for himself. He journeyed in curious books with brave companions on high adventure. He rode with Chaucer on a bright April morning over the hills toward Canterbury and listened to each embroidered tale with wonder and delight. He wandered with Una and her guardian lion in the haunted wood of Spenser's *Faërie Queene*. He followed the Pilgrim's progress and watched Christian and Apollyon in awful combat.

In Isaiah he read, "How beautiful upon the mountains are the feet of him that bringeth good tidings, that publisheth peace. . . ." His heart was glad with Jeremiah, singing, "The Lord hath appeared of old unto me saying, Yea, I have loved thee with an everlasting love: therefore with loving-kindness have I drawn thee." There was comfort and safety in the words of Isaiah: "For the mountains shall depart, and the hills be removed; but my kindness shall not depart from thee, neither shall the covenant of my peace be removed. . . ."

He heard Job as he mourned and talked with God in the land of Uz. He stood with John on Patmos, seeing a mighty angel standing in the sun; and his eyes grew bright with the secret beauty and wisdom that only children and angels know.

Mrs. Blake was in the kitchen, preparing supper. Mr. Blake had closed the shop for the day and was, as usual, reading in the next room. One by one the children had come in from play—Catherine, James, John, and Robert—all except twelve-year-old William. That boy! It's high time he was back, thought Mrs. Blake.

Suddenly he burst through the door and into the room. He was sunburned and tousled, and his hands were full of wildflowers.

"They're for you, Mother. I picked them over the river in the fields," he said, panting, as he kissed her.

"How lovely, and thank you," she said, and added, "So that's where you've been all day."

"Yes, I went all the way across Westminster Bridge and into the country beyond, as far as Dulwich. When I got tired I lay down under a tree. It was an old oak tree and while I was watching the sun through the leaves I noticed way up in the top branches something bright and shining. I thought it was a bird at first, but when I looked more closely I saw it was an angel, and in a moment the whole tree was full of them, with their wings bright and shining. It was the most beautiful sight I ever saw."

His mother looked at him sharply for a moment. "Why, that sounds very interesting," she said. "Tell me some more about them."

Mr. Blake looked up from his book. "You have seen no such thing," he said sternly.

"But I have indeed!" cried the boy indignantly. "I saw

them as plainly as I see you, and they were smiling at me."

"I will not have you telling lies." His father spoke angrily. "I shall punish you for this."

"Don't talk nonsense, James," interrupted Mrs. Blake. "You read to him this very morning out of the Bible about angels, where it says, 'For he shall give his angels charge over thee, to keep thee in all thy ways.' Perhaps it would do you good to see a few angels yourself some time. Why don't you try to understand what he means?"

"I won't have him telling lies," Mr. Blake persisted. "If he keeps this up he will turn out to be a chronic liar. The next time he does this I shall give him a beating."

"I can't help seeing them, and I *am* telling the truth," protested William. "And I hope I see them again," he added defiantly. "They made me very happy."

His father took him roughly by the shoulder.

"James!" Mrs. Blake spoke firmly. "Don't do it! Don't you know how children are? Some children will look out the window and see a dog and tell you they saw a tiger in the yard. You *know* Will is like that. Why can't you be sensible?"

"Oh, well! All right! All right!" Mr. Blake replied more gently. "I suppose you are right, as usual. But sometimes I just don't know what to make of the boy."

Later, when young William was in bed and his mother had come in to say good night, she paused by the bed and, looking down at the cherubic face, said, "You didn't finish telling me about those angels you saw today. What were they like, exactly?"

"We-ell, you see," he said slowly, "they aren't like people

—they're like—like *beings*, like thoughts, happy and shining, and they make you feel good."

Mrs. Blake thought for a long moment and said, "Yes, I see. That's just what they are—thoughts—good thoughts from God. They are His angel messengers, and may they watch over you tonight and always, son." And she leaned down and kissed him.

"I hope I shall always see them, and hear them too. Good night, Mother dear," said William Blake sleepily.

Nowhere does the spring come so dancingly over the hills as in England. The blossoming trees and flowers, the sheep in the meadows, and the cloud sheep in the cobalt sky called to William, and he laughed for pure joy and answered them.

As bright visions danced through his mind he found that one word called and another answered, and the thoughts and the words blended and flowed in a gay rhythm and cadence of verse.

He wrote these poems down and kept them, with the vague thought that someday he would make books with pictures of his own. His mind was filled with images that flowed like music, sometimes in words, sometimes in lines and colors, images sharp and clear and full of light.

In the cloud processions of the summer sky he saw shining figures of laughing children, and the beauty and joy of it overflowed in his heart, and later he made songs about them.

> Piping down the valleys wild,
> Piping songs of pleasant glee,

On a cloud I saw a child,
And he laughing said to me:

"Pipe a song about a Lamb!"
So I piped with merry chear.
"Piper, pipe that song again;"
So I piped: he wept to hear.

"Drop thy pipe, thy happy pipe;
Sing thy songs of happy chear:"
So I sung the same again,
While he wept with joy to hear.

"Piper, sit thee down and write
In a book, that all may read."
So he vanish'd from my sight,
And I pluck'd a hollow reed,

And I made a rural pen,
And I stain'd the water clear,
And I wrote my happy songs
Every child may joy to hear.

Exploring the city streets, William found the print shops and glued his nose to their windows, fascinated by this curious world engraved so perfectly in sharp detail. Paintings could be seen only in the mansions of the very rich, but prints could be bought in the shops for a few shillings. Prints were the people's picture gallery. As he studied them closely he could see that some were better than others, and he groped to find the reason why. He remembered the names of the artists whose pictures he especially admired. He recognized familiar scenes from the Bible whose stories he knew so well, and he learned the names of the artists who had made them—Michelangelo and Raphael, Fra Angelico and Dürer. There were engravings in which the eye could wander through strange landscapes, where every tree and rock was marvelously clear. Curious beasts moved among the trees; towered castles rose on rocky peaks; and bridges and steep-roofed towns clustered above broad rivers winding into far distances.

There were prints of "The Knight, Death and the Devil," a grim and terrifying vision; and there was one called "Melancholy," dreaming and mysterious; and another of Adam and Eve, naked, listening to the beguiling serpent in the Garden of Eden. These were by young William's favorite artist, Albrecht Dürer.

There were pictures by the famous Mr. William Hogarth, taken from the London street life that swarmed around him. These subjects were pictured in a series of scenes which told a story, like a play—"The Industrious Apprentice," "Marriage à la Mode," "The Harlot's Progress," and "The Rake's Progress." And there were grim views of "Gin Lane" and "Beer Street." These pictures taught lessons and preached sermons more powerfully than words could do.

So young Blake's mind became a picture gallery of the great masters of art in which line and color and sumptuous form were remembered and treasured for future use.

Sometimes the family went on a holiday to the Southwark Fair, where the jostling crowd gaped at the marvels and heard the din of hawkers. Horns, drums, and bagpipes filled the air. Here William once saw a great tiger, brought from far-off India, in a cage. He gazed into the staring golden eyes of the huge cat, wondering at the grace and power of the lean, striped body; and he kept the image in his poet's mind for its time.

Looking at the boy's drawings and verses, his parents talked of his future and prayed to know what was best for his happiness and success. He had been sent to a Latin school, where the average children of respectable trades-men usually went, to have numbers and the classics drilled into them, but he had returned rebellious and deeply dis-turbed by the ordeal.

If the sensitive boy was really determined to be an artist, his parents were willing to stand behind him with sympathy and understanding, though this was a hard decision for a middle-class tradesman to make at that or any time. When his father and mother at last agreed that he should go to drawing school, Blake was happy and grateful.

CHAPTER II

Engraver's Apprentice

Without Unceasing Practise nothing can be done.
Practise is Art. If you leave off you are Lost.

In spite of, or perhaps because of, his visions, young Blake was a sensible boy overflowing with health and energy. Just now he was interested in learning to draw, at Mr. Pars' Drawing School in the Strand. Here was a collection of plaster casts of Greek statues. His father bought him plas-ter casts of "The Gladiator" and "Hercules" for models to draw from at home. Drawing from "the antique" was at that time considered the basis of the artist's craft, but it was a discipline calculated to take all the imagination out of the most romantic boy. William spent long hours among the Greek gods, copying the plaster anatomies of Venus, Hercules, and Apollo until he could draw with sharp precision the bulge of each bone and muscle and fit together the architecture of the human frame.

After four years at Pars' Drawing School he had mastered the most useful tool of an artist. He had learned to draw the human figure. His father thought that the career of a painter was too uncertain, and that it would be more practical to become an engraver. William agreed. Together they went to see one of the most popular engravers in London.

Walking home from the interview, William was silent.

"What did you think of Mr. Ryland?" asked his father, breaking the silence.

After a long pause the boy said abruptly, "Father, I don't like the man's face. It looks as if he would live to be hanged!"

"Why, what a dreadful thing to say! He's a very respectable man. You should never say such things," said Mr. Blake.

"I can't explain. But I do know it is so," replied William doggedly.

Twelve years later Mr. Ryland was condemned on a forgery charge brought against him by the East India Company and was duly hanged.

It was in the shop of James Basire, a well-known engraver of the old school of precise and severe craftsmanship, that William began his seven years' apprenticeship.

His father gave him a little money when business was good, and Blake hoarded it to spend at Colnaghis's, the art dealer's. He learned by looking closely at the lines of a print to tell the difference between an etching, a dry-point, an engraving, an aquatint, and a mezzotint. He haunted the auction rooms where prints were sold. Sometimes a beautiful engraving by one of his favorite masters would sell for a price almost low enough for him to buy.

He became great friends with Mr. Abraham Langford, the auctioneer. When a lot of prints came up that might go cheap, and that the boy especially wanted, Mr. Langford would take William's bid and then say, "Going, going, gone! Sold to the gentleman in the rear," so fast that no one else could get in a bid. It became a game that they both enjoyed hugely. In time the boy owned a collection of fine prints.

Copperplate etchings and engravings were made in Europe to reproduce the great paintings of the masters, to illustrate books, and to reproduce popular subjects painted especially for engraving. In the eighteenth century, engraving had attained the perfection and beauty of a great art. Metal plates were often etched with acid; but the more difficult way was to take the bare copperplate and with a sharp steel burin cut or engrave the lines directly in the metal. It required great skill to manipulate the burin so that the thin lines would be just deep enough and the heavy ones would not be dug too deeply into the copper. When the engraving was finished, the plate was heated and coated with a thick ink worked with a dauber well into all the lines, and then the surface was wiped clean with rags. The damp paper that was to take the impression was laid on the inked plate, which was then pulled through a hand press. Very slowly and evenly the heavy rollers of the press were turned and the sheet carefully pulled from the plate. If each one of these hand skills had been performed just right, the print glowed and sparkled in all the richness and depth of black on white. Each clean line stood out in sharp relief. A perfect impression had been "pulled."

Mr. Basire's shop was an interesting place for the new apprentice, in spite of the long hours and the many tasks. William was really learning to be a print-maker as he ground the stiff ink or worked it into the deep lines on a copperplate, or damped the paper, or tacked down a wet impression so that it would dry out perfectly smooth. Mr. Basire was an exacting but kind master, and William was an industrious apprentice.

One day Mr. Basire called him into his office and told him that he could begin to cut a sample plate with the sharp little burins. It was a proud and exciting moment. In a short time the young Blake made all the blunders and mistakes possible—and learned how to correct them. Soon his strong wrist could cut a clean stroke of just the right length and depth. All day long he concentrated his energy on the sharp point of the burin as it plowed through the smooth copperplate, line by line. His clean line and sure modeling often made his engraving better than the original drawing he was copying. Sometimes he dreamed of how he would engrave his own designs, his visions of angels and prophets. He would cut them in detail, just as he saw them. He would make designs suggested by the great poets he knew so well—Chaucer, Milton, and Job—and he too would write great poems to go with his own designs.

Distinguished visitors came to Basire's shop; famous antiquarians, poets, print-collectors, and publishers looked over Blake's shoulder as he worked. Sometimes a shabby little man with a receding chin and bulging forehead came to the shop. He was the famous doctor, Oliver Goldsmith, whose poem *The Deserted Village* had delighted England, and whose play *She Stoops to Conquer* had been a huge success. To William's eyes Dr. Goldsmith's pock-marked face was beautiful, illuminated by the soul of a great poet.

CHAPTER III

In the Abbey

Prayer is the Study of Art.

The young apprentice became a devoted admirer of his master. Mr. Basire's motto was "Firm strokes and clear outlines," and this became loyal William's religion in art. For two years he was happy with the joy of a workman who loves his craft. Mr. Basire insisted on perfection, and everyone in his shop was proud of doing his job well. Harmony reigned.

As business increased, Basire needed more help. He engaged two new apprentices. On their first day in the shop they quarreled and got into a fight. Basire thrashed them both, but this only drove the row underground. In the peaceful shop that had run so smoothly things began to go wrong. Tools were lost, proofs were spoiled, and Blake, for the first time since he had started working there, began making errors on his plates.

He was sensitive to the atmosphere about him, and the demons of discord, in the shape of the quarreling apprentices, tormented him. It seemed his angels had departed, and now he needed a few very badly. He was becoming unhappy and discouraged.

One morning Mr. Basire called him into his private office. A severe reprimand from the old master is in order this time, thought William.

"I have here a letter from the Society of Antiquarians ordering a set of engravings of the antiquities in Westminster Abbey and other ancient churches," said Basire. "It is an important order, and, as you know, the drawings must be accurate and highly finished, and of course must be made on the spot." He cleared his throat and looked at William severely. "You, Mr. Blake, are the best draftsman in this shop. Indeed, I may say you are the best draftsman in any shop in London. I am assigning you to make these drawings and have arranged for your free access to the Abbey for as long as necessary.

"No objections, I presume," he added dryly, as he put the letter in his desk drawer.

"N-none at all, sir," stammered William. "In fact, I consider it a very great honor." He distinctly saw two small white wings sprouting from Mr. Basire's shoulders, and for a moment a faint halo encircled the stern engraver's head.

Blake stood alone in the vast, mysterious nave of Westminster Abbey. The slender columns reached up into pointed arches in the dim vault far above. Tall, sculptured angels smiled mysteriously at him, and grotesque faces carved in wood and stone grimaced at him from the shadows. Stone knights in armor and their ladies lay stiffly on their tombs, their feet resting on little dogs or lions. For centuries kings who had here been crowned in pomp and grandeur had been buried within these walls.

Most of the time Blake was alone. Occasionally a group

of visitors would be conducted through the Abbey by a verger. One day from his perch in a high gallery Blake watched a number of workmen engaged in some unusual business around an ancient tomb. This was strange, for it was a place where little had been touched or changed through the long centuries of stillness.

Directly beneath him, men with crowbars began removing the great slab that covered the tomb of King Edward the First, the most sacred spot in the Abbey. A shaft of light from the stained-glass windows fell across the open tomb. There lay robed in faded splendor the embalmed body of the saintly king who had been laid to rest seven centuries before. On his head was the golden crown, and in each hand a scepter. The sunken face still bore the character of feature which Blake had copied from the carved effigy on the tomb. For a moment it seemed that the living presence of the great monarch filled the vault with awesome majesty. Then, quickly the workmen rolled back the slab. The mysterious visitors left the Abbey and the wondering boy perched aloft amid its shadows—unaware that the Society of Antiquarians had obtained royal permission to open the tomb of Edward the First for purposes of historical research.

Blake was sixteen when he began making the drawings in Westminster. For the next five years he haunted the great Abbey and the ancient churches in and near London, constantly making careful drawings of Gothic carvings and architectural detail. He spent long hours alone in quiet sanctuaries, drinking in the beauty of the elongated sculptured forms of saints and kings and the glowing color of stained-glass windows.

He studied and copied the masterpieces of the medieval

craftsmen in all their richly fashioned detail. He breathed in the spirit of Gothic art and saturated himself in its mysterious harmonies. In silence, meditation, and long reflection he explored the invisible worlds of the imagination. He learned to listen with the inward ear and to see with spiritual vision. His "friends in eternity" showed him heavenly scenes, and his angels dictated poems that he saw and heard.

In the winter months, when it was too chilly to draw in the cold churches, he worked in Basire's shop at engraving plates from his drawings. Laboriously he perfected his craftsmanship with the burin.

While thoughts and ideals of art were taking place in his mind, in the world of material affairs he was mastering a practical and useful trade. He was still very young and as yet unsure, but he was aflame with imagination and energy, and he would follow his star wherever it led.

"Exuberance is Beauty!" he cried.

CHAPTER IV

Glad Day

. . . I will not Reason & Compare: my business is to Create.

There had been an odd character about London for some time, an American who came from Philadelphia. He was a printer who wrote almanacs, a natural philosopher who tinkered with curious contrivances and experimented with a strange, invisible "fluid" called electricity. He had been

sent to London by the Pennsylvania Assembly to annoy the
heirs of William Penn, who as owners of that colony, were
interested only in squeezing more taxes out of the reluctant settlers. Other American colonies which were having
similar difficulties with the British government had made
him their representative in London, until he had come to
represent in total the American cause in the growing differ-
ences with the mother country.

The man's name was Benjamin Franklin. He had made
friends as well as enemies among the most powerful men
in Britain. His difficulties were increasing as the Colonial
quarrel worsened. He was becoming rather a nuisance to
the king's ministers. Recently he had been publicly de-
nounced at a gathering of the most powerful lords in England at a hall called the Cock Pit. At any moment the government might arrest him on a charge of treason. When he
sailed for America it was not an hour too soon for his safety.

London was buzzing with news of the uprising in New
England. It would, of course, in the opinion of the Tories,
be quickly crushed by His Majesty's troops. But as the uprising turned into revolution there were many in England
who believed that the farmers fighting behind the stone
fences of New England and freezing at Valley Forge were
fighting for British liberty as well as American—in fact, for
all mankind. There were Englishmen who thought that the
king's party, which hired Hessian soldiers to shoot down
the American colonists, was as much the enemy of freedom
in Britain as it was in America.

This was a cause that captured Blake's imagination. In
his heart the bells of liberty were ringing. He had finished

his seven years as an engraver's apprentice. He was at last his own man. He was stirred by the writings of Voltaire and Rousseau, of Tom Paine and Thomas Jefferson, who were turning over the world and breaching old walls with their pens. A new age was being born.

Like most young artists of the time he began an historical picture for the Royal Academy exhibition. It was a painting in water color, and he was anxious to show all he knew of drawing figures and drapery. He rather expected that it might create something of a sensation. When it was done, he stood back, squinting at it with his head on one side. Really not bad, he thought.

The painting was good enough to be accepted for the exhibition, but it was hung, unfortunately, in the vestibule, where it received very little notice. It did not set the world on fire.

He realized that he was at heart against all academies and their stupid rules of art. Their exhibitions were full of dull portraits and hackneyed subjects from ancient history and the classics. He despised them. "Any fool can copy nature," he said.

He went to his easel and drew from imagination a nude figure of a youth with flaming hair and arms outstretched, standing on a mountaintop, one foot barely touching the earth. Rays of light radiated from his body and filled the sky. He called the picture "Glad Day."

The artist stood back and looked at it. This was not mere drawing; it was something more. It was inspiration! He knew it was dictated from on high by his angels. He was a scribe under orders. His business was to transcribe for mortal eyes the visions of a celestial imagination. "Glad Day" was his message to the world: "Here I am, William Blake—and nobody else!"

But he still lived in the material world and must eat, and wear clothes and pay for them. So for the time being he turned back to earth, and his engraver's trade, with high hopes.

He made an engraving of "Glad Day" and from time to time pulled prints and colored them by hand. This was his own personal style—something people would recognize even without his signature.

He was getting paying work from the publishers, to engrave illustrations for books from other artists' designs, which he was glad to do; for this was the craft he had mastered to make a living. When no one would employ him, then he could employ himself with his own "inventions."

"If a man is master of his profession, he cannot be ignorant that he is so; and if he is not employed by those who pretend to encourage art, he will employ himself, and laugh in secret at the pretences of the ignorant, while he has every night dropped into his shoe, as soon as he puts it off, and puts out the candle, and gets into bed, a reward for the labours of the day, such as the world cannot give, and patience and time await to give him all that the world can give."

CHAPTER V

My Kate

I told my love, I told my love,
I told her all my heart,
Trembling, cold, in ghastly fears—
Ah, she doth depart.

On Ludgate Hill in the heart of the old city—the one-mile-square City of London—rose majestically the great dome of St. Paul's Cathedral, designed and built by Sir Christopher Wren after the Black Plague and the Great Fire had terribly ravaged the city.

From here, Fleet Street and the Strand followed the great right-angle bend of the river to Charing Cross, called the center of London. Just south of this landmark stood the Houses of Parliament, close by the new Westminster Bridge. Directly behind them were the ancient Westminster Abbey and St. James Place, with its green park.

Westward, up the river, little rural villages that would in time be swallowed up by the growing city—Battersea, Chelsea, Hammersmith—nestled on the flower-strewn banks of the Thames.

London Bridge crossed the river to Southwark and the lovely cathedral where Chaucer's pilgrims set out on their storied way to Canterbury. London was mellow with a thousand years and more of turbulent history. From cellars to garrets the fast-growing city teemed with humanity. In winter the white fog crept in and veiled the streets and squares

Carnegie Public Library
Robinson, Illinois

with vagueness and mystery, but in the golden sunshine of spring the markets and fairs were gay, and at all times state processions, public hangings, fires, and mob rioting enlivened its robust citizenry.

Though Blake lived almost all his life in the midst of this swarming city and observed keenly and with feeling all its human episodes, he kept for himself and for his art that personal world of vision and imagination that was so peculiarly his own.

Another artist and genius just Blake's age was recording this human comedy with rollicking gusto. Thomas Rowlandson's prints, water colors, and caricatures were crowded with the opulent figures of London life in all its joys and dilemmas, made ridiculous by the robust humor of his lively pencil.

These two above all others expressed in great pictorial art, one in the spirit, and the other in the flesh, the genius of the English race in all its splendid exaltation and exuberant earthiness.

In 1780 political trouble-makers had set afloat religious propaganda that spread and flamed among the lower classes, exploding into the wild hysteria of mob violence (these uprisings are known as the Gordon Riots). The riffraff of Beer Lane and Gin Alley came out of their underworld and the miserable crawled from their cellars, burning and pillaging the houses of the wealthy. For six days and nights the sky glowed red with flame, and barricaded streets echoed to the firing of the soldiery on the rioters. Blake was carried along with the mob rushing toward Newgate Prison. The jail was stormed and burned, and the prisoners were released. After the frenzy had subsided somewhat, the king's soldiers took over, and then the savage vengeance of the law in trials and punishment. Hangings and quarterings were made a spectacle for the public benefit. The bodies of eight boys, all under fourteen, swung from the gibbet at Tyburn. "I never heard boys cry so," remarked an unusually tenderhearted spectator who had watched the hangings. These grim scenes haunted Blake's memory long afterward. He painted flames and red skies in the background of many of his pictures.

Although these tragic scenes left a deep impression on Blake, he was outwardly a gentle-spoken and mild-mannered young man who was beginning to make friends and enemies among the young artists and engravers of his own age in the artistic and literary circles of London. There was the young sculptor, John Flaxman, who was so classic in his taste and whose cold and pure drawings in outline of the Greek gods and goddesses Blake admired. In 1782 Flaxman introduced him to the eccentric Swiss artist Henry Fuseli, whose sharp wit and keen mind recognized kinship in Blake's rebellious genius, and they became lifelong friends. He also met Thomas Stothard, the fashionable historical painter.

His new friends recognized his abilities and were glad to put opportunities in his way. It was Fuseli who slyly remarked, "Blake is a good man to steal from."

Fuseli, too, was a visionary painter as well as an accomplished draftsman. His pictures were fantastic and imaginative—his dramatic painting called "The Nightmare" created a sensation—but they did not have the spiritual beauty and originality of Blake's designs.

Young Blake had an artist's eye for a pretty girl, and in particular the pink and blond beauty of one special girl—

saucy Polly Wood. She liked to laugh at him and tease him, but would not take him seriously; she was too practical to consider him as a husband. It was his first love affair, and he was terribly in earnest. When she favored other young men Blake became desperately jealous. "Do you think I am such a fool as to *marry* the likes of you?" she said, laughing mockingly at his proposal.

Deeply depressed and discouraged by her rejection, Blake moved from his old lodgings and took a room in the house of William Boucher, a market gardener. He hardly noticed his landlord's daughter Catherine when she first came into the room where he so often sat dejectedly. She had looked strangely at him and suddenly gone out. Later as they sat and talked together Blake told her of his sad love affair and how bad he felt about Polly. Catherine said impulsively, "I pity you from the bottom of my heart." This was so comforting to the unhappy young man that he looked at her for a long moment and said, "Then I love you for that." He suddenly realized that she was very good to look at. Her dark hair and eyes, the firm mouth and finely shaped head, seemed calm and cool and very lovely. He was amazed that a girl could be so unlike Polly and yet be so beautiful. In fact, at that very moment he completely forgot that there ever was such a person as Polly.

He saw Catherine almost every day. There was more to her than mere exterior prettiness. She was simple, sincere, and generous-minded, and she was above all a good listener, which was a great comfort to an egoist. Like most girls of her time, she could neither read nor write, for in those days education for women was frowned on, though well-bred horses and dogs were highly trained. But Catherine's ready intelligence, gentleness, and steadfast goodness were enough for William Blake. She was a quick learner, and William delighted in instructing her in the visionary world of a poet-genius.

It seemed very natural that soon they both should be deeply in love. But they wisely agreed that it would be best to wait one year. Marriage was a serious matter, and he wanted to be absolutely sure that she was the right one. As if *she* hadn't been sure the first time she saw him, when she entered the room and a prophetic realization had told her that he was to be her husband! It had been decided then forever for loyal, generous Catherine Boucher.

So Blake bent over his graver and copperplates, working at journeyman's jobs, saving his money, and thinking about Catherine. But the world was so full of pretty girls that sometimes he vaguely wondered how he was to know that any particular one was the right and only one. However, as the weeks and months slowly passed, Catherine's sweet face continued to haunt his thoughts. There was no doubt about it any more: she *was* the one.

When the year was up they were married at the new church in Battersea, close by the old river, on a bright Sunday in August. When they came to sign the parish register Catherine carefully marked an X, for she could not write her name.

Together they were beginning a long journey. The road would not be always smooth and level, but over mountain-tops and through dark valleys. There would always be a star in the darkness, burning sometimes bright and sometimes dim; but always together they would follow its light.

CHAPTER VI

Starting Out Together

I have Mental Joy & Mental Health
And Mental Friends & Mental wealth;
I've a Wife I love & that loves me;
I've all but Riches Bodily.

William was twenty-five and Catherine twenty-one when they started housekeeping in the lodgings at 23 Green Street on pleasant Leicester Square. The great Hogarth had lived nearby, and on the Square was Sir Joshua Reynolds' fine house, containing his famous picture gallery.

Sir Joshua was the most fashionable portrait painter of his day. His *Discourses* to his students were published and became a sort of Bible of art. The wealthy, the powerful, the fashionable people of the day flocked to his studio to have their features portrayed for posterity, for a portrait by Reynolds was a passport to immortality. Stately, solemn, and dull, their features would be venerated by countless generations.

Reynolds stood for everything in art that Blake despised. He referred to him as "Sr Joshua & his Gang of Cunning Hired Knaves." "This Man was Hired to Depress Art," he wrote. Blake expressed an equally savage contempt for Titian, Rubens, Correggio, and Rembrandt. They were daubers and bunglers, he said, because, "The great and golden rule of art, as well as of life, is this: That the more distinct, sharp, and wiry the bounding line, the more perfect the work of art, and the less keen and sharp, the greater is the evidence of weak imitation, plagiarism, and bungling. . . . How do we distinguish one face or countenance from another, but by the bounding line and its infinite inflexions and movements? . . . What is it that distinguishes honesty from knavery, but the hard and wiry line of rectitude and certainty in actions and intentions? Leave out this line, and you leave out life itself; all is chaos again, and the line of the Almighty must be drawn out upon it before man or beast can exist. Talk no more then of Correggio, or Rembrandt, or any other of those plagiaries of Venice or Flanders. . . ."

Though Blake had not previously thought much about such things, it was plain that he would now have to pay bills and provide the human necessities. He must make his living as an engraver in the bustling, practical city of London. Earning a living is sometimes a difficult problem for poets and artists, but Blake was a master of a useful craft, and he had no doubts. When there was little money or none, he and Catherine still felt abundantly rich in the wealth of companionship, youth, and beauty.

In the mornings he was up at six; he would build the fire and have the kettle boiling before Catherine was awake. She could make a shilling go a long way in the public markets, and her meals were well cooked and tasty.

She could not always follow him into the farthest reaches of his visionary world, but she listened understandingly to his accounts of celestial adventures, and believed. She brought patience and courage and faith to strengthen Blake's soaring spirit. She was to be tempered and tried in the fiery ordeal of the genius whose life she was to share.

Blake soon taught her to read and write. She quickly learned the many skills of the printer's art, and her deft hands became sure in the exacting details of the printer's craft. She soon became a valuable assistant in his arduous calling.

In spite of their humble origins, the young couple was accepted in the social and artistic world of the city. They began to be invited to dinners and evening parties, where soft candlelight shone on elegantly paneled walls and fops in silk coats and "small clothes" (knee britches), embroidered vests and lace trimmings, paid court to women upholstered in voluminous petticoats and vast powdered wigs, who flirted and simpered behind painted fans.

They were an attractive and vivacious pair, Catherine shapely and handsome, Blake short and broad-shouldered, with dark eyes, set far apart, that glowed and blazed under his massive forehead. His sharp wit sparkled and crackled, and his curious ideas often had a sudden and startling impact on the gossipy chatter of the crowd of poets, painters, and patrons who made up the intellectual world of London.

There were times when William spent days and nights of continuous painting and writing, until the larder became empty and Catherine had not even a shilling to stretch. At such times she would, without saying a word, simply put an empty plate before her husband when he sat down to supper. This saved arguing about money matters. He would take the hint and humbly go back to making engravings for the publishers for money.

He drew his pictures without models, but when anatomical structure or the flowing action of a figure blurred in his mind, Catherine would pose for a flying spirit or lend the fresh beauty of her young body as a model for a willowy Eve. "You are Eve," he said once, looking up piercingly from his drawing to verify the image in his mind by the visual form of Catherine's loveliness.

With other young artists and poets, the Blakes were invited to the evening gatherings of the celebrated Mrs. Henry Mathews. She was a lady of wealth and intelligence who assembled at her "reunions" men of reputation in the arts, rising young talents, poseurs, savants, eccentrics, writers, musicians, and tedious dullards who fluttered around the flame of her ego. To all promising talents the doors of her house, 27 Rathbone Place, were open.

Mrs. Mathews, with Mrs. Sarah Siddons, the tragic actress; Angelica Kauffmann, the portrait painter; and Hannah More, the poet and writer, were only a few of the brilliant women of the new Age of Reason, of Invention, of the Machine, and of Liberty that was rising out of a changing world as the eighteenth century drew to a tumultuous close. Men in Britain were beginning reluctantly to admit that women had minds.

It was Mrs. Mathews who had discovered the boy genius Flaxman. Learned as well as elegant, she would read Homer in Greek to the sculptor, interpreting as she went, while the boy sat by her side, sketching an illustration for a passage here and there.

Mr. Blake enlivened these evening gatherings by singing a number of his poems to music of his own composition. These lyric verses had been written when he was in his teens. There was freshness and originality in their simple music. Mrs. Mathews was enthusiastic. Flaxman proposed that the poems should be printed, and Mrs. Mathews offered to pay for half of it (Flaxman, though he could ill afford it, shared the cost) and persuaded her husband, who was a distinguished clergyman, to write an apologetic introduction, in the fashion of the times. Dr. Mathews wrote that he hoped "their poetic originality merits some respite from oblivion" and apologized for the author's absence of leisure, "requisite to such a revisal of these sheets as might have rendered them less unfit to meet the public eye." The introduction was not so much an apology as a masterpiece in depreciation.

Blake began to come less often to Mrs. Mathews' intellectual evenings. He felt humiliated by Mrs. Mathews' patronage, and the artificial atmosphere and silly chatter of her stuffy evenings was becoming unbearable. Gossipy ladies found it disconcerting to listen to an intense young man seriously report that he had recently attended a fairies' funeral and who told of having just had a pleasant evening's conversation with Socrates and the prophet Isaiah. Beneath his mild, soft-spoken manner there was something that blazed and shone like a comet going by.

The sheets of collection, called *Poetical Sketches*, were badly printed and presented to Blake, to have bound at his own expense and to give away to his friends. But he made no effort for their sale. His sensitive feelings had been deeply offended by the vulgar condescension of the parson's introduction to his poems. He would work out some way to print and decorate his poems, and he wanted to write others and make them into books, beautifully decorated and illuminated with his own designs.

Fuseli had introduced him to Joseph Johnson, the radical, free-thinking publisher who attracted to his circle the rebellious critics of the government and the friends of liberty. Johnson gave Blake several commissions for engravings, and Blake began to attend the Johnsons' weekly dinners, held over his bookshop in St. Paul's Churchyard. Here the talk was stimulating, exciting, and dangerous. Here he felt happy and at home.

Blake designed and engraved for Johnson six plates to illustrate *Original stories from real life with conversations calculated to regulate the affection and form the mind to truth and goodness,* by Mary Wollstonecraft. Blake thought the illustrations were as dismal as the text. Such books were popular at the time as a form of torture inflicted on defenseless childhood.

There was another bookshop in St. Paul's Churchyard. Over the door was a sign that read "Juvenile Library." This was an entirely new idea in the book business, and Mr. John Newbery, the bookseller, put an advertisement in the *London Chronicle* for December 1765, which read: "On the first of January, being New Year's Day, Mr. Newbery intends to publish the following important volumes, bound and gilt, and hereby invites all his little friends who are good to call for them at the *Bible and Sun* in St. Paul's Churchyard, but those who are naughty to have none."

The last part of this ad may have lost Mr. Newbery a lot of customers; nevertheless, the new idea of books of their very own for children flourished. He wrote many of the books himself and provided them with lots of pictures. "He called himself the friend of children but was the friend of all mankind," wrote his friend Oliver Goldsmith.

His son Francis carried on the bookshop after him and continued to publish books for children. Blake, in passing the sign of the *Bible and Sun,* stopped before the window and looked closely at these "little penny books radiant with gold and rich with bad pictures"; for his mind was radiant with books of his own containing poems about children, and he would take care that the pictures too would be as radiant as the poems.

CHAPTER VII

Robert

When the doors of perception are cleansed, everything will appear to men as it really is, infinite.

The "songs of innocence" were changing to the "songs of experience," as Catherine and William courageously faced the struggles and problems before them. Two years after their marriage, his father died. The devout old dissenter had been a stern parent, but he had given his son understanding and wise guidance. He had gone as far with him along his strange path as his plebeian shopkeeper's intellect could follow.

Death drew the family together for the moment. Blake's elder brother, James, took over the house and the hosiery shop at Golden Square. Though he too had the Blake visionary streak in him, he was a shopkeeper at heart and had little understanding or sympathy for his poet brother. For the youngest brother, Robert, William had a deep affection.

The William Blakes moved into the house next door to the house on Broad Street, and Robert, who was five years William's junior, came to live with them. On the first floor William started a print shop in partnership with James Parker, who had been an apprentice with him at Basire's. The atmosphere was harmonious and business was good. William worked hard at engraving orders for book illustrations. When there was time he worked on his own pictures and sent them to the Royal Academy, where they were sometimes accepted and exhibited, though without creating any special notice.

Although his subjects were often taken from the Bible, they were not literal illustrations but interpretive designs. He called these pictures his "inventions," for they were visions from imagination and not scenes in the "vegetable world," seen only by dull mortal eyes. Robert became his pupil and made sensitive designs in his brother's style that delighted William, although the younger man did not master the iron discipline of drawing in line.

Catherine, with two dreamers to care for, had her hands full. When Robert unconsciously occasioned some domestic mishap for the hundredth time, long-suffering Catherine would lash out at him with a bit of tiger in her tongue. Robert would take these sallies meekly enough.

Once William, in the next room, overhearing an interchange of this sort, rushed furiously into the room and shouted at Catherine, "Kneel down and beg Robert's pardon directly, or you will never see my face again!"

Catherine actually got down on her knees and took it all back. "I beg your pardon; I am in the wrong."

By this time the amazed Robert was boiling too, and roared like a true English gentleman, "Young woman, you lie. *I* am in the wrong!"

For a moment the three glared at each other in silence. The situation was absurd. Then Catherine smiled sheepishly and rose. Robert grinned. All three burst out laughing and were good friends again.

For three years the brothers shared a close and affectionate companionship. When Robert, at the age of twenty-five, fell ill of a hopeless malady, hanging for weeks between life and death, William watched by his bedside day and night, as if by his presence he could hold off the Grim Reaper.

At the last moment, when dark doors opened and strange light gleamed for a moment through shadowy curtains, William said he saw Robert's bright soul ascend in light, saw him clap his hands in joyful release. For three days and nights William himself lay in a stupor of grief and exhaustion.

Robert left a notebook containing a few of his sketches. William kept this memento, and during the years filled both sides of its fifty-eight leaves with poems, sketches, and ideas, until it became a crowded treasure house of his inmost thoughts and visions.

The image of Robert remained alive and near in William's thoughts. An encompassing love held them united in spiritual communion. He would speak of Robert as if nothing had happened; indeed, Blake's spirit was strengthened with renewed faith in all that they had shared together of beauty and truth. He said that Robert often came to him in his sleep and they talked of art.

"I cannot think of death as more than the going out of one

room into another," he said to himself, and was deeply comforted.

CHAPTER VIII

A New Process

. . . I defy any Man to Cut Cleaner Strokes than I do, or rougher where I please, & assert that he who thinks he can Engrave, or Paint either, without being a Master of drawing, is a Fool.

After Robert's death Blake dissolved his partnership with Parker and moved to 28 Poland Street, a short distance away.

He collected his songs and poems. He had often read and sung them to Catherine and Robert, and they had enjoyed and praised them.

There were "Laughing Song" and "Piping Down the Valleys Wild" and "The Lamb," "The Little Boy Lost" and "The Little Boy Found" and "The Little Black Boy," "The Ecchoing Green" and "A Cradle Song." There were others too—all were simple and joyous verses about children, for children, written out of a child heart. He called them *Songs of Innocence.*

Blake now planned to make them into a book with pages illuminated by his own designs. He would engrave text and pictures so they would have unity and beauty and be just the way he saw them in imagination. If no one would publish the book he was determined to find some way to do it himself. But how? There were mechanical problems that would have to be worked out. The question kept running in his mind, and he groped for an answer.

He still had the sheets of poetry which Mrs. Mathews had had printed so enthusiastically for him. "The Poetical Sketches, by W.B., London, 1783," the title page read; and there was that dreadful preface by the parson. His *Songs of Innocence* must never look like this!

As he lovingly handled the little gleaming copperplate on his work table, the lines of the songs and rhythms of design danced across it like fire. There should be color, with perhaps touches of gold. But books at this time were set in cold type and were printed with proper margins and dismal prefaces, and bound in leather with gilt edges.

At night Blake would wake in the darkness. With the material world obscured from him, his own thoughts stood out in bright clarity. One night the answer came; he knew how to make the plates for the *Songs of Innocence*. Early the next morning he told Catherine that he had the whole process for printing his poems worked out. It seemed as if Robert had appeared to him in a dream and explained the new process to him. He sent Catherine out to buy materials —a little asphaltum, varnish, and acid—with their last half-crown. When she came back he dipped a small drawing brush in the varnish and drew on the copperplate a slim nude figure playing with a dancing child in swirling lines. He painted the back of the plate solidly with the varnish and dipped it in the acid bath until the exposed copper was eaten away, leaving the figure he had painted in varnish standing out in high relief. When he pulled a print from the little plate, the impression was clear and sharp. He had invented a new process—a perfect method for reproducing the "Songs." It was neither engraving nor line etching. At a later time the process became widely used, and it is now called "relief etching."

Blake made twenty-seven small plates for the book, each about three by five inches, in this manner. Around the hand-lettered text of the poems were woven flowing designs. After he and Catherine had richly hand-colored the printed sheets with water colors of Blake's own making, Catherine deftly sewed the sheets in board bindings. The exquisite designs and delicate color harmonies woven through the text were in perfect accord with the music of each tender lyric.

It was a perfect thing. As the happy artist kissed Catherine he said that his angels had sung the songs but that it was the spirit of Robert who had showed him the way to print and engrave them, and that his Kate had been a wonderful helper.

From time to time he printed single sheets or bound and colored copies on the order of friends, gratefully accepting the price but reluctant to speak of money matters. The sales of prints from these plates provided them with part of the meager income that kept them barely clothed and fed through the years. They both believed absolutely in the mystical Biblical economy of the providing ravens and the daily manna, and throughout their long pilgrimage their simple needs were always met. They never had to accept charity.

Only a few copies of the *Songs of Innocence* were printed, and few of these have survived. Although the pages have been reproduced by modern mechanical processes, the rainbow beauty and magic of Blake's handiwork is lost, for the "dark Satanic Mills" of mechanical reproduction cannot transmit their subtle beauty.

CHAPTER IX

Memorable Fancies

One Law for the Lion & Ox is Oppression.

Blake's newly invented process of relief etching held un-limited possibilities. His mind flamed with ideas and inventions, visions, fancies, and epic poems dictated by his friends in eternity, to be engraved and printed in the new relief method.

He wrote and engraved a new poem, with designs on seven plates about four by six inches, which he printed, colored, and called *The Book of Thel*. In the poem a very abstract damsel named Thel, the youngest of the daughters of the Seraphim, holds a philosophical dream conversation with a lily, a cloud, a worm, and a clod of earth. The poem begins with questions.

> Does the Eagle know what is in the pit?
> Or wilt thou go ask the Mole?
> Can Wisdom be put in a silver rod?
> Or Love in a golden bowl?

Blake hand-colored the illuminated pages in prismatic harmonies that are like the stained-glass windows of cathedrals. The figures float in the vast universe of space—a universe on a postcard.

But the dictation of his friends in eternity was not always sweetness and light, for they now began to transmit the awful mysteries of Good and Evil. Blake called his next book *The Marriage of Heaven and Hell*.

As usual, the text of the twenty-four engraved pages was in script writing illuminated with inventions richly hand-colored. The book begins with an "Argument," followed by a few remarks by "The Voice of the Devil," concluding with the statement that "Energy is Eternal Delight." This is followed by a report from the infernal regions, which he calls "Proverbs of Hell." These have a bitter crackle, as of flames, and a mystical, half-hidden wisdom that is sharp and cutting:

Listen to the fool's reproach! it is a kingly title!
What is now proved was once only imagin'd.
The weak in courage is strong in cunning.
To create a little flower is the labour of ages.
The busy bee has no time for sorrow.
You never know what is enough unless you know what is
  more than enough.

Exuberance is Beauty.
A fool sees not the same tree that a wise man sees.
If the fool would persist in his folly he would become wise.
The tygers of wrath are wiser than the horses of instruction.
He who has suffer'd you to impose on him, knows you.
When thou seest an Eagle, thou seest a portion of Genius;
  lift up thy head!
The most sublime act is to set another before you.
One thought fills immensity.

Accompanying the maxims of Hell are several "Memorable Fancies." These are vivid and diabolic episodes with hidden meanings, such as:

As I was walking among the fires of hell, delighted with the enjoyments of Genius, which to Angels look like torment and insanity; I collected some of their Proverbs; thinking that as the sayings used in a nation mark its character, so the Proverbs of Hell show the nature of Infernal Wisdom better than any description of buildings or garments. . . .

I was in a Printing house in Hell, & saw the method in which knowledge is transmitted from generation to generation.

In the first chamber was a Dragon-Man, clearing away the rubbish from a cave's mouth; within, a number of Dragons were hollowing the cave.

In the second chamber was a Viper folding round the rock & the cave, and others adorning it with gold, silver and precious stones.

In the third chamber was an Eagle with wings and feathers of air: he caused the inside of the cave to be infinite; around were numbers of Eagle-like men who built palaces in the immense cliffs.

In the fourth chamber were Lions of flaming fire, raging around & melting the metals into living fluids.

In the fifth chamber were Unnam'd forms, which cast the metals into the expanse.

There they were receiv'd by Men who occupied the sixth chamber, and took the form of books . . . arranged in libraries.

The Marriage of Heaven and Hell was a work that smelled strongly of brimstone, and its style had the scorched and flickering majesty of "Infernal wisdom."

CHAPTER X

Tom Paine, the Rebellious Needleman

The Inquiry in England is not whether a man has talent and genius, but whether he is Passive and Polite and a Virtuous Ass, and obedient to noblemen's opinions in art and science.

There was engraved on the rim of the great bronze bell of the Philadelphia Statehouse the words of the Book—to "proclaim liberty throughout all the land unto all the inhabitants thereof . . ." The clamor of its tolling had reached across the Atlantic and was waking peoples from centuries-old bondages. A new age was being born, and the old order was shattered and falling in flame and blood.

The people of Paris had risen, shouting, *"Liberté, Egalité, Fraternité!"* Mobs from the dark slums and dank cellars of the city had taken the Bastille, the terrible government prison, and freed the prisoners.

When the news reached London, Blake had put on a red cap, the *bonnet rouge* of the Revolution, and had boldly walked through the streets of his city with a defiant swagger. Of course, he had written a poem. It was called *The French Revolution*, in seven parts; Joseph Johnson had set up in type the first part, but it was not actually published.

The fall of the Bastille was a brief moment of triumph for the Sons of Liberty in England. Then came the news of the terrible September (1792) massacres. The French revolutionists had taken vengeance on the aristocrats.

In England a wave of horror swept over the people. Blake

flung the red cap and the six unpublished parts of *The French Revolution* into the fire. The next year (1793) the head of King Louis the Sixteenth fell heavily into the basket under the guillotine, as that of King Charles had fallen under the ax in England over a hundred years before.

Tom Paine—"the rebellious needleman," as the Tories called him—the famous pamphleteer, had come to London from America, where his pen had served mightily in the fight for freedom. Joseph Johnson had invited Paine to speak at one of his famous Tuesday-evening dinners. Blake was there, aglow with excitement as he listened to the great man. He was anxiously aware that such fearless speaking at this time could lead straight to the Tyburn gibbet, and he remembered uneasily the Gordon Riots and the hangings. Although Paine had just been made a citizen of France and elected to the National Convention, Blake knew that this would be of no help.

After the speech Paine's friends received news that government agents were secretly waiting for him at his lodgings. Blake insisted that Paine must leave at once for France. It was a matter of life or death, and there was not a moment to lose. Funds and luggage were provided, and in an hour the pamphleteer was on the road to Dover.

The boat for Calais with Mr. Paine aboard had been gone but a few minutes when the government's agents arrived with a warrant for his arrest. For once Blake had appeared for a moment on the great stage of history.

Joseph Johnson was sentenced to jail for selling a seditious book. Here he continued to hold the "Tuesday dinners" for his literary friends, which they enjoyed immensely —in spite of the somewhat cramped surroundings!

PART TWO

Lambeth

(1793-1800)

Bring me my Bow of burning gold:
Bring me my Arrows of desire:
Bring me my Spear: O clouds unfold!
Bring me my Chariot of fire.

I will not cease from Mental Fight,
Nor shall my Sword sleep in my hand
Till we have built Jerusalem
In England's green & pleasant Land.

CHAPTER XI

Lambeth

*He who does not imagine . . . in stronger and better
light than his perishing and mortal eye can see, does not
imagine at all.*

It was spring, and Catherine was restless with a woman's
longing for a house of her very own. Blake too felt the call
of the outdoors and the country lanes, of the open fields
that lay across the new Westminster Bridge. Their rooms
in Poland Street, where they had lived for six years, were
filled with portfolios bulging with prints. All the litter of
writing, engraving, printing, and housekeeping left them
hardly room to turn around. Across the river lay the suburb
called Lambeth, and here the Blakes found a suitable house
and moved their belongings, including the heavy hand press
for which Blake had paid forty pounds.

The new home was Number 13 in a group of residences
called the Hercules Buildings. These were solid, fortress-
like little dwellings of brick, each with a small respectable
front garden and in the rear the kind of neat private greens-
ward where the British family likes to sit in seclusion.

To the south lay the country, "England's green and pleasant land," calling them through winding lanes and over
the green hills. From the rear windows they could see the
towers of Westminster Abbey across the river, gleaming

Carnegie Public Library
Robinson, Illinois

silver in the morning mist. Their new home had the quiet of the country and yet was within walking distance of the city.

However prosaic had been the atmosphere of the Hercules Buildings, from now on Number 13, at least, was to be enlivened with visions and splendor.

There were the innumerable company of angels that came and went, and Bible prophets and ancient poets—among them Milton, Chaucer, and Shakespeare, who occasionally dropped in for an evening's chat with Mr. Blake (so he said). Blake told of seeing in visions the majestic figure of an old man with a flowing mane who appeared frequently at the head of the stairs in the twilight. Dark, driving clouds swept round him as he leaned out of a flaming sun and reached down one long arm, which held a gigantic compass, to strike the circle of the earth. Of this grand conception Blake made one of his noblest designs. From the plate of it he made prints which he loved to color again and again. He called this picture "The Ancient of Days Striking the Circle of the Earth with Golden Compasses."

To friends who could understand, Blake sometimes explained that spiritual visions were not seen by the material eye, but that the artist who saw them must draw them with clarity and detail to satisfy and convince the material eye.

. . . The Prophets describe what they saw in Vision as real and existing men, whom they saw with their imaginative and immortal organs; the Apostles the same; the clearer the organ the more distinct the object. A Spirit and a Vision are not, as the modern philosophy supposes, a cloudy vapour, or a nothing: they are organized and minutely articulated beyond all that the mortal and perishing nature can produce. He who does not imagine in stronger and better lineaments, and in stronger and better light than his perishing and mortal eye can see, does not imagine at all. The painter of this work asserts that all his imaginations appear to him infinitely more perfect and more minutely organized than any thing seen by his mortal eye. Spirits are organized men. Moderns wish to draw figures without lines, and with great and heavy shadows; are not shadows more unmeaning than lines, and more heavy? O who can doubt this!

Blake's friends became accustomed to his odd habit of speaking of characters out of the past who came to his imagination through his reading as if they had actually visited him in person. But outsiders who heard this talk circulated rumors of his insanity, and gossip of his madness began to go about the town. When questioned by unsympathetic or merely curious people, Blake became annoyed and perversely made even more exaggerated fanciful statements.

When asked about ghosts, he said they were low, vulgar creatures seen only by unimaginative people. Just once had he himself seen one. He was standing in the door to the garden, enjoying the twilight, when he noticed it coming down the stairs—a grim, grisly customer, making right for him—and he had quickly taken to his heels. No doubt he *saw* the ghost (illusion) clearly enough—saw his own fear, which he visualized as a terrifying image; and he also knew well enough that, like his prophetic visions, this was not a material fact. He understood that men easily believe what they see, but that they do not so easily, but just as certainly, see what they believe.

Catherine was supremely happy in having for the first time a house of her own. Their worldly affairs were prospering and they could for a while even afford a servant. Catherine made the house and garden a welcome spot for the London friends who came over Westminster Bridge to visit her husband and inspect the work that was pouring furiously from his hand and brain. When she was not helping with the printing, coloring, and binding of the new books, she would sit for hours, knitting, in the little wainscoted room where Blake worked by the window under a screen of transparent paper, which engravers use to diffuse the light.

At Lambeth he printed "Songs of Experience." These were twenty-seven exquisite lyrics he wrote to accompany the *Songs of Innocence*—a sequel that balanced light with dark, joy with sadness, and the sweet music of childhood with the bitter stab of experience. "The Chimney Sweeper," "The Little Vagabond," and "A Little Boy Lost" are charged with heartache for the doomed children of the London slums.

There are tenderness and beauty in lovely Lyca and her mystic adventure among the strange beasts in "The Little Girl Lost."

> Sleeping Lyca lay
> While the beast of prey,
> Come from caverns deep,
> View'd the maid asleep.
>
> The kingly lion stood
> And the virgin view'd
> Then he gamboll'd round
> O'er the hallow'd ground.

Leopards, tygers, play
Round her as she lay,
While the lion old
Bow'd his mane of gold

And her bosom lick,
And upon her neck
From his eyes of flame
Ruby tears there came;

While the lioness
Loos'd her slenderness
And naked they convey'd
To caves the sleeping maid.

The poem "The Tyger" has become the most famous of all his writings. All that is splendid and savage in Blake's imagination flames forth in

Tyger! Tyger! burning bright
In the forests of the night,
What immortal hand or eye
Could frame thy fearful symmetry?

The plates were about four by six inches in size and were printed together with the *Songs of Innocence* in one volume of fifty-four pages. Blake's engraved announcement of the book read:

SONGS OF INNOCENCE AND OF EXPERIENCE
Shewing the Two Contrary States of the Human Soul
Etched 1789–1794

The pages were richly colored by Blake's own hand and the price was thirty shillings. He was thirty-six when he published the songs. This was the end of his youth. He never again would evoke the fresh beauty, the joy and sorrow of a child's world, as he had done in the tender melodies of these simple verses.

CHAPTER XII

Prophetic Books

The children of their new neighbors at the Hercules Buildings took a shy interest in Catherine and William Blake; and when it became known that Blake was an artist they were curious and excited.

Blake took special notice of them, and soon they were saying good morning and asking about one another's health, and first thing they knew they were friends. Occasionally Catherine would make a cake and ask them in to tea. Most exciting of all, Mr. Blake sometimes invited his young friends to see his workroom and to look at his pictures. He would ask what they thought of this picture or that, and when they told him all the things they liked about each one, he was immensely pleased.

The poet and the children understood each other perfectly. Children, he knew, were on the side of imagination. They were always a great comfort—especially when Blake made some illustrations for the Reverend John Trusler, who had written a book with the horrible title *The Way to Be*

Rich and Respectable. Mr. Trusler did not like Blake's drawings because he could not understand them. He claimed that "the Visions of Fancy are not to be found in This World."

Blake wrote the minister a letter in which he explained his mistake. "To Me This World is all One continued Vision of Fancy or Imagination, & I feel Flatter'd when I am told so. . . .

"But I am happy to find a Great Majority of Fellow Mortals who can Elucidate My Visions, & Particularly they have been Elucidated by Children, who have taken a greater delight in contemplating my Pictures than I even hoped. Neither Youth nor Childhood is Folly or Incapacity. Some Children are Fools & so are some Old Men. But There is a vast Majority on the side of Imagination or Spiritual Sensation."

If one or two were on his side, Blake claimed that it was a vast majority—on the principle that one on God's side is a majority. Children were on his side, and he was on theirs. Children didn't need explanations. They recognized delight when they saw it. They just looked and enjoyed.

"Fun I love," he wrote, "but too much Fun is of all things the most loathsom. Mirth is better than Fun, & Happiness is better than Mirth. I feel that a Man may be happy in This World. And I know that This World Is a World of Imagination & Vision."

He began work on what he called his "Prophetic Books," meaning not that they foretold the future but that they were epic poems that told of spiritual adventures.

The first of these was a little volume of seventeen plates called *For the Sexes: The Gates of Paradise.* The titles were illustrated with seventeen small etchings or emblems, symbols of earth, air, fire, and water. "I Want! I Want!" and "Help! Help!" pictured ideas and questions in "the lost Traveller's Dream under the Hill."

Following this, Blake wrote and engraved *Visions of the Daughters of Albion.* The pages of this book were decorated with ariel figures woven into the text in a way that made the page a window through which the reader looks into space. It was a poem of great beauty, though obscure meaning.

As his poetry became more abstruse to the uninitiated, the pictures became more vivid and rainbow-hued. The script of the text hung in iridescent veils of color. The designs glowed with beauty and spiritual excitement, blending in perfect harmony.

Blake's theme was the eternal struggle between good and evil, reason and the imagination, spiritual freedom and material bondage, light and darkness. The characters in the Prophetic Books were mighty figures of abstract and changing meanings to whom he gave strange names. The lines thundered with the roarings of Rinthral, the writhings of Urizen, the howlings of Albion, the groanings of Los, and the shudderings of the Daughters of Beulah.

The designs among which the script was set were a pictorial drama charged with the beauty and mystery of a celestial ballet moving against backgrounds of suns and flame, of red and yellow skies, and of seas of midnight blue or soft gray-greens.

Friends bought a few copies of the Prophetic Books. For a hundred years they lay forgotten in odd corners of England. Today they are the treasures of the great libraries and museums of England and America.

The flaming skies and crashing worlds of Blake's imagination, and the roaring giants that writhed and struggled in its murky heights and depths, were no more violent than the scenes that were shaking the outer world beyond the quiet garden of 13 Hercules Buildings.

Like other Englishmen, Blake listened anxiously to the news of revolts, of war, and of bloodshed across the English Channel as the century drew to a close.

In America the Colonies had declared and won their independence and were bound together by a great Constitution into a nation "conceived in liberty." For eight years the great hero of liberty, George Washington, had served majestically as the first president of the Republic.

But Blake, as he daily walked the streets of London, saw the wretched chimneysweeps and children of the gutter for whom there was no hope. He had written in anguish:

> I wander thro' each charter'd street,
> Near where the charter'd Thames does flow,
> And mark in every face I meet
> Marks of weakness, marks of woe.
>
> In every cry of every Man,
> In every Infant's cry of fear,
> In every voice, in every ban,
> The mind-forg'd manacles I hear.

His heart ached. His mind, seeking for some sense of meaning and reality in this outer chaos, found refuge in imagination, and tormented visions poured out in wild poems whose meaning was clear only to himself. Interwoven with the lines on each page he engraved frenzied figures that moved in a cosmic dance of rhythmic beauty and grandeur.

But if the contents of his long mystic poems seemed incomprehensible, they were visually thrillingly beautiful.

Blake finished the last of the Prophetic Books in 1795. The months of concentration on the small plates, of all his nervous energy focused on the point of a small graver, had been a physical ordeal. But his mind was still full of pictures. For relaxation he drew in tempera on millboard a series of "inventions." Printing while still wet, he could get several impressions of the same plate. These he enriched with hand coloring and mossy textures. The prints were larger and freer in handling than the engravings, and are some of his noblest conceptions. Among these are "Elijah in the Chariot of Fire," "Hecate," "Nebuchadnezzar," "Pity," and the allegorical "Newton."

If many of the subjects for his pictures were taken from the Bible, this was because he read it continually, and his art, philosophy, and life were steeped in it. He searched its depths and heights and found truth. Like a true Protestant, he interpreted it according to his inner light and found his union with God without a human intermediary.

"The Old & New Testaments are the Great Code of Art," he said.

CHAPTER XIII

Young's Night Thoughts

*"Dear Sir, excuse my enthusiasm or rather madness, for
I am really drunk with intellectual vision whenever I take
a pencil or graver into my hand . . ."*

Blake, in a frenzy of concentrated energy, had created nine
Prophetic Books in a period of three years. Sometimes he
awoke in the night and wrote and drew till dawn, with
Catherine sitting beside him. He counted on her to be
there when he returned from his visionary world, and she
never failed in keeping the long night watch by the side of
the possessed man. "My Kate" he called her; and she always
spoke of him as "Mr. Blake." "I never saw Mr. Blake's
hands idle," she said. "When he was not reading, he was
always working."

There were times when they took holidays and went on
long walks over the hills into the Arcadian countryside. They
would talk to the shepherds and watch the playful lambs,
or perhaps stop at a farmhouse to take shelter from a passing
shower. They would eat a hearty supper at a country inn and
trudge home in the long summer twilight, watching a new
moon rise over the hill. Blake would sing his songs, holding
Catherine's hand, his heart full of deep content.

To make money he cheerfully undertook odd jobs of
hack engravings for now-forgotten books. He engraved fourteen plates from the drawings by the author to illustrate A

Narrative of Five Years' Expedition among the Revolted Negroes of Surinam.

Among the dismal and dull poems which so appealed to the popular taste of the day was a book known as *Night Thoughts,* by Edward Young. An enterprising bookseller of New Bond Street, Richard Edwards, undertook the ambitious project of issuing a new, illustrated edition in folio size (a sheet folded once), in four parts. There were to be nine hundred pages. On most of these the text was to be set in an elaborate design that occupied most of the page.

In a blaze of enthusiasm Blake created five hundred and thirty-seven designs in water color. Each page was dynamic with a swift and flowing beauty of line. Swirling figures flew in mystic traffic between earth and sky. Primeval giants seized and hurled down blazing suns, and elongated figures rushed through space in spiral rhythms, their anatomies contorted into swift and incredible foreshortenings.

The plates were the largest that Blake had ever engraved for a book, but by the end of the year he had completed forty-three plates for Volume One. When this was printed, he colored several copies in harmonies as rich and as subtle as the designs themselves.

Later Mr. Edwards came with the sad news. The book was not selling. There was no possibility that it would. He could not afford to go on with the project. Already there had been a heavy financial loss. Blake's designs were too bold, too original, for the insipid taste of the day, which delighted in the soft and sentimental prettiness of the Italian engravers. The respectable Londoner was not prepared to be lifted into the infinite void by Blake's visions and to dance amid an innumerable company of angels in the whirling cosmos of eternity. Mr. Edwards kept the designs and paid Blake a few pounds for the year's labor. So conspicuous a disaster in the publishing world discouraged other publishers from employing Blake.

He had counted on the project for artistic success and material prosperity. Instead it proved a crushing reversal of his hopes and dreams.

CHAPTER XIV

"Dear Friend of My Angels"

*"As to Myself, about whom you are so kindly Interested,
I live by Miracle. I am Painting small Pictures from the
Bible."*

Although friends and visitors came to the Blakes' home in the Hercules Buildings, not many were buyers—except Mr. Thomas Butts. Butts was a prosperous, respectable merchant who lived in fashionable Fitzroy Square. He was peculiar only in that he devoted the time and interest that most English gentlemen of his class spent with horses, dogs, and foxes to the society of artists. He had been attracted to Blake in 1793 and was interested in his ideas and in his poems and pictures. He called regularly once a week on Tuesdays.

These were pleasant visits, enriched with elevating discussions of art and religion, and Mr. Butts often bought and took home with him a picture. He was perfectly satisfied with whatever Blake might choose to give him, and he always paid the artist one guinea—a sum on which the

Blakes could live for an entire week! For many years Mr. Butts' guinea was the only regular income the Blakes had. Catherine could make it go a long way, and the sense of security in Mr. Butts' weekly purchase was mentally worth a whole lot more.

In the course of a year Mr. Butts in this way spent some fifty guineas on "Blakes." This was considerably more than most of the well-to-do invested in art in a year or a lifetime, but Mr. Butts rightly felt that he was getting his money's worth. Soon his house in Fitzroy Square was filled from cellar to garret with Blake originals. Aside from the painter's own collection of his works, it was the best and only collection of Blakes in the world.

John Flaxman, the sculptor, whom Blake had first met many years ago at Mrs. Mathews' parties, had just returned to London from a seven years' stay in Italy. In a moment of enthusiasm Blake wrote, "You, O dear Flaxman, are a sublime Archangel, My Friend & Companion from Eternity . . ."; he addressed Flaxman as the "Sculptor of Eternity"! Flaxman was a Swedenborgian, and they were old friends. Flaxman had made a series of graceful illustrations in outline for Homer's *Odyssey* in a style somewhat based on the classic Greek vase paintings. These had been engraved in Rome by a popular Italian artist named Piroli, but the plates had been lost on the way to England, where the book was to be printed. Blake admired the drawings, and Flaxman commissioned him to engrave them for the book. Blake received five guineas for each plate.

It was Flaxman who, in 1800, introduced Blake to Mr. William Hayley, by way of further helping him to patronage and prosperity. Hayley was a poet and country gentleman famous principally for a grisly poem called *The Triumphs of Temper*. It had been a best-seller in England for twenty years. He was writing a life of the poet Cowper and had conceived the idea of helping a deserving artist with the commission to illustrate it. Mr. Hayley moved in the best society. He was eager to put work and patronage in the way of an artist who would come to Felpham, where he lived, and "set up shop." He proposed this to Blake.

The usual way to success for an artist was under the patronage of some aristocratic family, where he painted portraits, taught the children, and made himself generally useful and agreeable; in return, he met the "best people" and received the care and affection sometimes bestowed on a pedigreed dog.

Catherine and William Blake were both London born and bred, and a possible change to the country seemed a great event. To Blake, with his financial struggles, Hayley's offer looked like a godsend. In his ardent imagination the prospect blossomed with rosy possibilities. Catherine, too, was eager and excited at the idea of moving to Felpham. "My Wife," Blake wrote to Hayley, "is like a flame of many colours of precious jewels whenever she hears it named."

Blake wrote back to Mr. Flaxman:

We are safe arrived at our Cottage, which is more beautiful than I thought it, & more convenient. . . . No other formed House can ever please me so well; nor shall I ever be perswaded, I believe, that it can be improved either in Beauty or Use.

. . . My Wife & Sister are both well, courting Neptune for an embrace.

Our Journey was very pleasant; & tho' we had a great deal of Luggage, No Grumbling; All was Chearfulness & Good Humour on the Road, & yet we could not arrive at our Cottage before half past Eleven at night, owing to the necessary shifting of our Luggage from one Chaise to another; for we had Seven Different Chaises, & as many different drivers. We set out between Six & Seven in the Morning of Thursday, with Sixteen heavy boxes & portfolios full of prints. And Now Begins a New life, because another covering of Earth is shaken off. . . .

Thus Catherine and William and his sister rode over the Sussex Downs, changing chaises and the sixteen heavy boxes seven times, all with good humor, and arriving at the earthly paradise they had rented for twenty pounds a year in the little village of Felpham-by-the-Sea.

PART THREE

"My Three Years' Slumber on the Banks of the Ocean"

(1800-1803)

But if we fear to do the dictates of our Angels, & tremble at the Tasks set before us; if we refuse to do Spiritual Acts because of Natural Fears or Natural Desires! Who can describe the dismal torments of such a state!

CHAPTER XV

On the Banks of the Ocean

For the first time Blake stood upon the banks of the ocean, hearing the thunder of heavy surf on lonely beaches. On a day of driving wind and rain he would sometimes walk alone along the shore, bemused by the elemental battle of wild breakers crashing on the bastions of rocky headlands.

There were sunny days when he traced the dissolving patterns of sea foam on white sand. On still nights the moonlight fell, ghostly, on white cliffs, and the shining moon path led across dark waters to his feet.

All the seven seas were England's, and in Blake's inner ear echoed the thunder of the guns of Abukir as the broadsides from Nelson's frigates shattered Napoleon's fleet in the far-off Mediterranean and the hopes of the upstart Corsican to wrest India from Britain's grasp.

From the upper windows of the cottage in Felpham, Blake could see the ocean, and on the landward side the rolling Sussex Downs. He and Catherine often took long walks together by the sea. In the surge of breakers Blake heard new rhythms for a poem and in the curling surf saw visions of kings and prophets in solemn processionals.

He often accompanied Hayley on his daily ride. Blake's horse was a gentle animal named Bruno, who had been lent to him by a friendly patron, Mrs. Price. Hayley's mount was an army horse trained in surprising maneuvers. It was Hayley's peculiar habit when riding to carry an umbrella, against the rain and sun; once in the saddle, he would raise the umbrella, sometimes frightening the horse so violently that its rider landed in a ditch.

Hayley, who, through poor management, had lost possession of a large part of an inherited estate, had retired from the cares of the world and the burdensome applause of society to "a marine cottage with an embattled turret" which he had built and whose comfortable library he furnished with busts and pictures.

It was Hayley's kindly intention to keep Blake so occupied with commissions that he would abandon his unprofitable visions and become a successful and prosperous artist. One of his first jobs for Blake was a commission to paint a series of eighteen life-sized portraits of the poets from Homer to Haley as murals for his library. Blake also was engaged on illustrations for Hayley's writings, especially his life of Cowper.

In time Blake secured numerous orders for miniature portraits from the neighboring gentry, as he had easily mastered this new technique. He wrote to Thomas Butts:

Mr. Hayley acts like a prince. I am at complete ease. Sussex is certainly a happy place and Felpham in particular is the sweetest spot on earth. My present engagements are in miniature painting. Miniature has become a goddess in my eyes, and my friends in Sussex say that I excel in the pursuit. I have a great many orders and they multiply.

He taught drawing to the children of aristocratic families, but refused the offer to become a court painter for the Duke of Richmond.

As the lyric pattern of country living and the wonder of the mysterious ocean became more familiar, the excitement of the new scene wore off. The cottage was damp, and the atmosphere of the sleepy little society of Felpham and its environs was deadening to the imagination. Blake was a Londoner, and he missed the drama of the city, missed its crowds and pageantry. His well-intentioned patron referred to him condescendingly as "our good Blake, our excellent Blake, this good warm-hearted artist and this singularly industrious man." Although this was the usual attitude of a great patron toward his respected underlings, it was offensive to the pride of a poet-painter.

More and more, Blake was becoming aware of his humiliating function of hired companion to a dull literary country squire. Yet at the same time he was grateful to his amiable patron for the kindly interest in his welfare and the efforts to put him in the way of commissions. So he kept, on the surface, the pretense of the industrious underling-companion, but the angels and the tigers of imagination were growing restless.

He remembered how at one of Mrs. Mathews' dinners he had become so bored that he had suddenly turned to the highly respectable lady next to him and asked, "Did you ever see a fairies' funeral?"

"Never, sir!" she had replied indignantly.

"I have," he said, in the casual way he spoke of his visions. "I was walking alone in my garden; there was a great stillness among the branches and flowers and a more than common sweetness in the air; I heard a low and pleasant sound, and I knew not whence it came. At last I saw the broad leaf of a flower move, and underneath I saw a procession of creatures of the size and color of green and gray grasshoppers, bearing a body laid out on a rose leaf, which they buried with songs, and disappeared. It was a fairy funeral."

The lady had looked at him wildly and changed the subject, and Blake had smiled dreamily and become silent. He would not explain to her that fairies were the rulers of the vegetable world. They stood for the mysterious beauty of the flowers, the waving grass, the laughter of the leaves, the voices of the wind in bare treetops or of the thunder of surf on moonlit beaches.

Blake was much more at home and happier with these small creatures of his fancy than with Mr. Hayley or the other kind patrons of Felpham.

CHAPTER XVI

The Ram Horn'd with Gold

O thou Ram horn'd with gold
Who awakest from Sleep
On the Sides of the Deep.

One day a letter came from London to Blake in Felpham. It was from his faithful friend Thomas Butts. It contained among many warm expressions of amity a flowery poem that Mr. Butts had composed and dedicated especially to Mr. Blake in Felpham. It read:

. . . O May ye be allowed to chuse
For your firm Friend a Heaven-born Muse,
From purest Fountains sip delight

Be cloathed in Glory burning bright,
For ever blest, for ever free,
The loveliest Blossoms on Life's Tree. . . .

Blake was so pleased with this poetic confection that he answered immediately in his most flowery style:

Felpham, *Octr. 2d 1800.*

Friend of Religion & Order,

I thank you for your very beautiful & encouraging Verses, which I account a Crown of Laurels, & I also thank you for your reprehension of follies by me foster'd. Your prediction will, I hope, be fulfilled in me, & in future I am the determined advocate of Religion & Humility, the two bands of Society. . . . Receive from me a return of verses, such as Felpham produces by me, tho' not such as she produces by her Eldest Son; however, such as they are, I cannot resist the temptation to send them to you.

To my Friend Butts I write
My first Vision of Light,
On the yellow sands sitting.
The Sun was Emitting
His Glorious beams
From Heaven's high Streams.
Over Sea, over Land
My Eyes did Expand
Into regions of air
Away from all Care,
Into regions of fire
Remote from Desire;
The Light of the Morning
Heaven's Mountains adorning:
In particles bright

The jewels of Light
Distinct shone & clear.
Amaz'd & in fear
I each particle gazed,
Astonish'd, Amazed;
For each was a Man
Human-form'd. Swift I ran,
For they beckon'd to me
Remote by the Sea,
Saying: "Each grain of Sand,
Every Stone on the Land,
Each rock & each hill,
Each fountain & rill,
Each herb & each tree,
Mountain, hill, earth & sea,
Cloud, Meteor & Star,
Are Men seen Afar."

. . . . . .

My Eyes more and more
Like a Sea without shore
Continue Expanding,
The Heavens commanding,
Till the Jewels of Light,
Heavenly Men beaming bright,
Appear'd as One Man,
Who complacent began
My limbs to infold
In his beams of bright gold;
Like dross purg'd away
All my mire & my clay.
Soft consum'd in delight
In his bosom Sun bright

I remain'd. Soft he smil'd,
And I heard his voice Mild,
Saying: "This is My Fold,
O thou Ram horn'd with gold,
Who awakest from Sleep
On the Side of the Deep.
On the Mountains around
The roarings resound
Of the lion & wolf,
The loud Sea & deep gulf.
These are guards of My Fold,
O thou Ram horn'd with gold!"

The correspondence continued, and Blake reported at length all the details of life at Felpham. The letters recorded his gradual change of mood as he found that he was really a prisoner of a kindness, a convention, and a material success that was death to the imagination and to his art.

He wrote his views on art to Mr. Butts and said modestly:

. . . the Pictures which I painted for you Are Equal in Every part of the Art, & superior in One, to any thing that has been done since the age of Rafael. . . . I also Know & Understand & can assuredly affirm, that the works I have done for you are Equal to Carrache or Rafael, . . . or Else I am Blind, Stupid, Ignorant and Incapable in two year's Study to understand those things which a Boarding school Miss can comprehend in a fortnight. . . .

But you will justly enquire why I have not written all this time to you? I answer I have been very Unhappy, & could not think of troubling you about it, or any of my real Friends. (I have written many letters to you which I burn'd & did not send) . . .

Another letter contained a long visionary rhyme that revealed the tormented workings of his restless imagination:

> For double the vision my Eyes do see,
> And a double vision is always with me.
> With my inward Eye 'tis an old Man grey;
> With my outward, a Thistle across my way.
>
> . . . . . .
>
> Now I a fourfold vision see,
> And a fourfold vision is given to me;
> 'Tis fourfold in my supreme delight
> And threefold in soft Beulah's night
> And twofold Always. May God us keep
> From Single vision & Newton's sleep!

Occasionally Blake sent to Butts pictures he long had
promised, but more often he made excuses. His time, he
said, was taken up with the drudgery of hackwork for Hayley. Besides this, his angels in eternity had begun dictating
again—an immense work of the imagination.

But none can know the Spiritual Acts of my three years'
Slumber on the banks of the Ocean, unless he has seen them
in the Spirit, or unless he should read My long Poem descriptive of those Acts; for I have in these three years composed
an immense number of verses on One Grand Theme, Similar
to Homer's Iliad or Milton's Paradise Lost, the Persons &
Machinery intirely new to the Inhabitants of Earth (some of
the Persons Expected). I have written this Poem from immediate Dictation, twelve or sometimes twenty or thirty lines
at a time, without Premeditation & even against my Will; the
Time it has taken in writing was thus render'd Non Existent,
& an immense Poem Exists which seems to be the Labour of

a long Life, all produc'd without Labour or Study. I mention
this to shew you what I think the Grand Reason of my being
brought down here. . . .

Between his angels' dictation and Mr. Hayley's commissions his patience was wearing thin, and he wrote:

. . . but Mr. H. approves of My Designs as little as he does
of my Poems, and I have been forced to insist on his leaving
me in both to my own Self Will; for I am determin'd to be
no longer Pester'd with his Genteel Ignorance & Polite Disapprobation. I know myself both Poet & Painter, & it is not
his affected Contempt that can move me to any thing but
a more assiduous pursuit of both Arts . . . but his imbecile
attempts to depress Me only deserve laughter. . . . I shall
leave every one in This Country astonish'd at my Patience &
Forbearance of Injuries upon Injuries; & I do assure you that,
if I could have return'd to London a Month after my arrival
here, I should have done so, but I was commanded by my
Spiritual friends to bear all, to be silent . . . I have compell'd
what should have been of freedom—My Just Right as an Artist & as a Man. . . .

When the inevitable scene of conflict came and Blake
broke out in resentment against Hayley, his amiable patron
was amazed. He had been utterly unaware of the real man
and of the fierce spiritual struggle that had been taking place
within Blake for three years; and he was so astonished and
shocked at what seemed to him to be Blake's ingratitude
that he wept. Both of them lost their tempers. Accusations
flew back and forth. For some time after the quarrel they
did not speak.

But Blake could not remain angry long, and Hayley's
habitual good nature and kindliness toward the artist soon

revived. Catherine acted as peacemaker, and the two in-
compatibles were reconciled. It was agreed that they would
return to London with Hayley's blessing.

CHAPTER XVII

Sedition and Trial

O why was I born with a different face?
Why was I not born like the rest of my race?

While the Blakes were still in the pleasant cottage at Felpham an unusual episode occurred, so sinister in its possibilities that it threatened to bring Blake's career to a sudden
and tragic end.

Blake wrote an account of the adventure to Mr. Butts.

. . . I am at Present in a Bustle to defend myself against a
very unwarrantable warrant from a Justice of Peace in Chichester, which was taken out against me by a Private in Captn.
Leathes's troop of 1st or Royal Dragoons, for an assault & seditious words. The wretched Man has terribly Perjur'd himself,
as has his Comrade; for, as to Sedition, not one Word relating
to the King or Government was spoken by either him or me.
His Enmity arises from my having turned him out of my
Garden, into which he was invited as an assistant by a Gardener at work therein, without my knowledge that he was so
invited. I desired him, as politely as was possible, to go out
of the Garden; he made me an impertinent answer. I insisted

on his leaving the Garden; he refused. I still persisted in desiring his departure; he then threaten'd to knock out my Eyes, with many abominable imprecations & with some contempt for my Person; it affronted my foolish Pride. I therefore took him by the Elbows & pushed him before me till I had got him out; there I intended to have left him, but he, turning about, put himself into a Posture of Defiance, threatening & swearing at me. I, perhaps foolishly & perhaps not, stepped out at the Gate, &, putting aside his blows, took him again by the Elbows, &, keeping his back to me, pushed him forwards down the road about fifty yards—he all the while endeavouring to turn round & strike me, & raging & cursing, which drew out several neighbours; at length, when I had got him to where he was Quarter'd, which was very quickly done, we were met at the Gate by the Master of the house, The Fox Inn (who is the proprietor of my cottage), & his wife & Daughter & the Man's Comrade & several other people. My Landlord compell'd the Soldiers to go in doors, after many abusive threats against me & my wife from the two Soldiers; but not one word of threat on account of Sedition was utter'd at that time. This method of Revenge was Plann'd between them after they had got together into the stable. This is the whole outline. . . .

Give me your advice in my perilous adventure; burn what I have peevishly written about any friend. I have been very much degraded & injuriously treated; but if it all arise from my own fault, I ought to blame myself.

O why was I born with a different face?
Why was I not born like the rest of my race?
When I look, each one starts! when I speak, I offend;
Then I'm silent & passive & lose every Friend.

Then my verse I dishonour, My pictures despise,
My person degrade & my temper chastise;
And the pen is my terror, the pencil my shame;
All my Talents I bury, and dead is my Fame.

I am either too low or too highly priz'd;
When Elate I am Envy'd, When Meek I'm despis'd.

Catherine was terribly frightened—and indeed she might well be. The penalty for one adjudged guilty of treason was hanging; after which the body was drawn and quartered and the head and four quarters were hung up in public places as a warning. Sedition was one of the most dreaded charges that could be brought against a man.

The soldier, John Scofield, and his companion had brought charges of sedition against Blake under oath, and the trial was set for January 11, 1804. Hayley immediately came to Blake's assistance and contributed a hundred pounds toward his bail. Blake was confident that the testimony of his friends and neighbors who had witnessed the scene would acquit him.

He believed that the plot was instigated by the government to trap him because of his long-past association with Thomas Paine and other friends of liberty. In this case it was fortunate that Blake's writings were unknown. However, it *was* possible that in his anger he might have said something unflattering about the Royal Dragoons.

Blake was eager to get to work on *Jerusalem, The Emanation of the Giant Albion*, a poem he had begun in Felpham. Back in his native city, he was alive again. But Catherine was ill with anxiety over the impending trial. She remained in London when Blake returned to Chichester to be tried.

Several days before the trial Hayley had gone out riding, carrying his umbrella, as usual. When he opened it, the horse shied wildly and Hayley flew through the air, landing head down on a roadside boulder. Only his new high hat saved him from tragedy. While undergoing repairs he said earnestly to the doctor, "Living or dying, I must make a public appearance at the trial of our friend Blake."

The *Sussex Advertiser* of January 16, 1804 announced:

William Blake, an engraver at Felpham, was tried on a charge exhibited against him by two soldiers for having uttered seditious and treasonable expressions, such as "D—n the King, d—n all his subjects, d—n his soldiers, they are all slaves; when Bonaparte comes it will be cut-throat for cutthroat, and the weakest must go to the wall; I will help him, etc., etc."

At the trial Mr. Hayley, as the great man of the neighborhood, testified effectively for Blake. Young Sam Rose, whom Hayley had engaged as Blake's lawyer, was eloquent, and the poet's friends and neighbors who were witnesses testified to his innocence, mildness, and peaceableness. Anything Mr. Blake might have said about the Royal Dragoons was declared to have been provoked by the irritation of the moment. To the soldier's testimony, Blake had cried, "False!" with a ringing earnestness that thrilled the crowded court. After a long and tedious trial the jury brought in a verdict of not guilty. The courtroom cheered. Hayley was exultant; Blake was grateful; and the pair was entirely reconciled.

That night Mrs. Poole, Hayley's friend and neighbor, gave a dinner in honor of Blake and to celebrate the ac-

quittal. Old friends rejoiced together, and the evening overflowed with good cheer, toasts, speeches, and laughter.

In the coach returning to London, Blake fell into conversation with an old soldier and picked up a valuable bit of
information which he wrote back to Mr. Hayley.

I write immediately on my arrival, not merely to inform you
that in a conversation with an old soldier, who came in the
coach with me, I learned that no one, not even the most ex-
pert horseman, ought ever to mount a trooper's horse. They
are taught so many tricks, such as stopping short, falling down
on their knees, running sideways, and in various and innumerable ways endeavouring to throw the rider, that it is a miracle
if a stranger escape with his life. All this I learn'd with some
alarm, and heard also what the soldier said confirmed by another person in the coach. I therefore, as it is my duty, beg
and intreat you never to mount that wretched horse again, nor
again trust to one who has been so educated. . . .

Gratitude is Heaven itself; there could be no Heaven without gratitude; I feel it and I know it, I thank God and man
for it, and above all, you, my dear friend and benefactor, in
the Lord. . . .

PART FOUR

17 South Molton Street

(1804-1821)

"What," it will be Question'd, "When the Sun rises, do you not see a round disk of fire somewhat like a Guinea?" O no, no I see an Innumerable company of the Heavenly host crying, "Holy, Holy, Holy is the Lord God Almighty." I question not my Corporeal or Vegetative Eye any more than I would Question a Window concerning a Sight. I look thro' it & not with it.

Carnegie Public Library
Robinson, Illinois

CHAPTER XVIII

The Return

*I doubt not yet to make a figure in the great dance of life
that shall amuse the spectators in the sky.*

Blake's return to London from Chichester after the trial was
a return to life and liberty. He had been acquitted of the
charge of high treason, and freed from Hayley's patronage;
he exulted in this double liberation.

In London the Blakes secured a first-floor lodging at Number 17 South Molton Street—only a mile from his birth-
place. This was to be their home for seventeen years.

The old friendship with Mr. Hayley revived more easily
at long range, and the two men exchanged affectionate letters again. In fact, so sugar-coated did Blake's recollections
of Felpham become that he wrote Mr. Hayley:

Remembering our happy Christmas at lovely Felpham, our
spirits still seem to hover round our sweet cottage and around
the beautiful Turret. I have said "seem," but am persuaded
that distance is nothing but a phantasy. We are often sitting
by our cottage fire, and often we think we hear your voice
calling at the gate. Surely these things are real and eternal in
our eternal mind, and can never pass away. My wife con-
tinues well, thanks to Mr. Birch's Electrical Magic, which she
has discontinued these three months.

But in his private notebook, where he sometimes recorded his less noble feelings, he scrawled:

My title as a Genius thus is prov'd;
Not Prais'd by Hayley nor by Flaxman lov'd.

. . . .

To Hayley
You think Fuseli is not a great painter. I'm glad.
This is one of the best compliments he ever had.

Hayley had loaded Blake with errands in London, and details of publishing, and he practically became Hayley's business agent. Blake's letters at this time were fawning and flattering. Perhaps he felt he owed this to Hayley for his testimony in his behalf at the trial. Or perhaps he felt it was good business. Maybe he really meant it. His letters contained such effusions as, "O lovely Felpham, parent of Immortal Friendship, to thee I am eternally indebted for my three years' rest from perturbation and the strength I now enjoy"; and he wrote Hayley, "You can have no idea, unless you were in London as I am, how much your name is loved and respected."

In his private notebook he wrote:

I write the Rascal Thanks 'till he & I
With Thanks & Compliments are quite drawn dry.

Blake threw himself into the engraving of the hundred plates of *Jerusalem*. It opened with an address to the public that had the delightful blare of a circus calliope.

Sheep   To the Public   Goats
After my three years' slumber on the banks of the Ocean, I again display my Giant forms to the Public. My former

Giants & Fairies having reciev'd the highest reward possible, the love and friendship of those with whom to be connected is to be blessed. I cannot doubt that this more consolidated & extended work will be as kindly received. . . . Reader, forgive what you do not approve, & love me for this energetic exertion of my talent. . . .

The words he had scratched out left the remaining sentences unintelligible.

The text of the poem was a kaleidoscope of changing images and mystical chants in which whatever meaning Blake darkly hinted at was hopelessly concealed from the uninitiated. The designs in which the text was woven did not illustrate the poem in any external sense but were an accompaniment of monumental vision.

As Blake labored over *Jerusalem* he came increasingly to believe himself belonging to the race of Biblical prophets who had in past ages pronounced divine revelations to an unbelieving world.

He published another practically incomprehensible poem that he had conceived at Felpham. It was "a Miltonian poem in two books, the Author and Printer W. Blake." There were forty-five small pages exquisitely colored by hand with the usual grace of design. It is said that to appreciate great poetry one must be a great poet. Perhaps this is why so few have understood Blake's Prophetic Books. But we can feel their strange, splendid images and the music of their majestic language. Like great music they may be enjoyed but not simply explained.

CHAPTER XIX

Mr. Cromek and The Grave

*When a base man means to be your enemy, he always
begins with being your friend.*

Mr. Robert Cromek had been an engraver of ability in
London for some ten years. During this time he had learned
that the business of publishing and selling engravings and
illustrated books was immensely more profitable than the
labor of engraving the copperplates from which the illustrations were printed. He had decided to go into the publishing business. His very first venture would have to be a
success financially, because he had very little capital to
start with or to fall back on.

Blake had shown him the designs he had made for a poem
called *The Grave* by the poet Robert Blair. This poem was
so elegantly dismal and discouraging that it had been read
and admired by a large book-buying public for many years;
but it had never been illustrated.

Cromek saw at once the commercial possibilities of an
edition illustrated with engravings from Blake's sensational
drawings. To promote this forthcoming book Cromek obtained and published a glowing endorsement of the "moral
value" of Blake's designs from ten prominent members of
the Royal Academy, including Flaxman and Fuseli and the
president of the Academy, Benjamin West. Best of all,

some friends had been able to secure the patronage of Queen Charlotte for the book. This exalted approval was probably not due to any special interest on the part of the aged queen.

Cromek paid Blake twenty guineas for the twelve drawings and closed the deal with the express promise, verbally given, that Blake should have the much-better-paid job of engraving the designs. As this would probably be several hundred pounds, the prospects looked bright for future comforts and security for the Blakes, who had been living on half a guinea a week.

When Blake heard that Queen Charlotte had graciously permitted the designs to be dedicated to her, he wrote a dedicatory poem.

To the Queen

The Door of Death is made of Gold,
That Mortal Eyes cannot behold;
But, when the Mortal Eyes are clos'd,
And cold and pale the Limbs repos'd,
The Soul awakes; and, wond'ring, sees
In her mild Hand the golden Keys:
The Grave is Heaven's golden Gate,
And rich and poor around it wait;
O Shepherdess of England's Fold,
Behold this Gate of Pearl and Gold!

He made a design to enclose the verses, but Cromek would not pay the four guineas Blake asked. Mr. Cromek meanwhile had changed his plans about the engraving of Blake's drawings. He had secured advance subscriptions to *The Grave* in the amount of £1800. It was now possible to engage a fashionable Italian engraver who would render Blake's designs in the soft mechanical technique which was so admired by the public. Cromek feared that the hard definition of Blake's rugged engraving would not be popular. He commissioned Sciavonnetti, the best engraver in the Italian style in London, to do the work. Even the shock of Blake's terrifying conceptions would be softened and cheered by the suave technique of the more favored engraver.

Cromek did not tell Blake of this arrangement; and when it finally reached Blake's ears he was very angry and deeply discouraged, but of course could do nothing about it. After all, the agreement with Cromek had not been in writing, and Cromek *had* bought and paid for the designs and copyright.

Cromek still remained on friendly terms with Blake. He, like others, found that snooping in the corners of Blake's studio was a great way of picking up ideas. During one of his visits he noticed pinned on the wall a drawing of Chaucer's "Canterbury Pilgrims." The poem had never been illustrated before, and Cromek saw another opportunity for a big profit. He offered to buy the drawing. This time Blake was wary and refused to sell. He said he intended to paint the subject and engrave it himself.

Cromek simply went to Blake's old friend Stothard, a skillful craftsman and a painter of uninspired historical illustrations—the stock-in-trade of British academic art. Without mentioning Blake's picture, he commissioned Stothard to paint the Canterbury pilgrimage for sixty guineas. At the same time he engaged Sciavonnetti to engrave it. Neither Blake nor Stothard knew of the other's relations with Cromek. On a friendly visit to Stothard's studio, Blake saw the painting. Stothard wanted to introduce Blake's head as one of the Canterbury pilgrims!

When Blair's *The Grave* was published Blake's name as illustrator was on the title page and his portrait appeared as a frontispiece. There was a flowery advertisement at the back of the book announcing the engraving of Stothard's "Canterbury Pilgrims." Blake was disgusted and furious with both Cromek and Stothard. He felt that he had been tricked out of two golden opportunities for fame and financial success—opportunities that would have lifted the bitterness of poverty for Catherine and brought recognition and opportunity to him as an artist. In his private notebook he wrote:

> C(romek) loves artists as he loves his Meat.
> He loves the Art, but 'tis the Art to Cheat.
> A petty Sneaking Knave I knew—
> O, Mr. Cr(omek), how do ye do?

But Blake had a persistent faith that the public would appreciate his work, in spite of all the evidence to the contrary. He made up his mind to hold a public exhibition of his paintings that would convince the world of his genius and forestall and defeat Cromek's plan for publishing Sciavonnetti's engraving of the "Canterbury Pilgrims."

CHAPTER XX

The Public Exhibition

Mr. B. appeals to the Public, from the judgment of those narrow blinking eyes, that have too long governed art in a dark corner.

April had come out of the south, and England's countryside was a bright tapestry of bloom and blossom and little singing birds. In London the genial sun had vanquished the winter fogs, black with coalsmoke. Again the streets were clamorous with the cries of venders and peddlers and the rattle of carts and wains over the cobblestones on their way to Covent Garden Market. Outside Blake's window a crowd collected around a Punch and Judy show, blocking the street, and angry draymen were bawling protests. The air was full of laughter and cockney banter. Spring had come to London.

For Blake every tree was full of singing angels and every cloud in the sky was teeming with infant pipers "piping songs of pleasant glee."

The season had affected Catherine with feminine unrest, and she was cleaning her husband's best black suit and scouring the winter's grime from walls and corners. "That's enough for today," said William as he tied on her bonnet and dragged her protestingly out the door into the languorous spring sunshine. They crossed the bridge and rambled through Southwark and on into the country beyond, for an afternoon's holiday.

In Southwark had stood the Tabard Inn, where the Canterbury pilgrims had made their early start on that April morning some three hundred years before. Blake's mind was full of Chaucer's poem, for he had been working for many weeks on a long panel portraying the famous company mounted and starting on their journey. From imagination he had sharply drawn each character with his clean and wiry line, including the horses and dogs and the landscape background. There had been a problem in accounting for the legs of all the horses and fitting them properly into the uninterrupted flow of the whole design. But finally every significant detail was lovingly recorded.

He wrote a catalogue of the exhibition in which he described at length each picture, beginning with the characters of the Canterbury pilgrimage. The announcement read:

A DESCRIPTIVE CATALOGUE

OF PICTURES, POETICAL AND HISTORICAL INVENTIONS, PAINTED BY WILLIAM BLAKE IN WATER COLOURS, BEING THE ANCIENT METHOD OF FRESCO PAINTING RESTORED: AND DRAWINGS, FOR PUBLIC INSPECTION, AND FOR SALE BY PRIVATE CONTRACT.

Blake wrote:

Of Chaucer's characters, as described in his Canterbury Tales, some of the names or titles are altered by time, but the characters themselves for ever remain unaltered, and consequently they are the physiognomies or lineaments of universal human life. . . . As Newton numbered the stars, and as Linnaeus numbered the plants, so Chaucer numbered the classes of men.

The Painter has consequently varied the heads and forms of his personages into all Nature's varieties; the Horses he has also varied to accord to their Riders; the costume is correct according to authentic monuments.

The Knight and Squire with the Squire's Yeoman lead the procession, as Chaucer has also placed them first in his prologue. The Knight is a true Hero, a good, great, and wise man; his whole length portrait on horseback, as written by Chaucer, cannot be surpassed. He has spent his life in the field; has ever been a conqueror, and is that species of character which in every age stands as the guardian of man against the oppressor. . . .

Number V in A *Descriptive Catalogue* was called "The Ancient Britons." This was the largest, most "historical" invention he had ever painted. It was a mythical battle scene, and the main figures were life-size. The scene was bathed in the blood-red light of a symbolically setting sun. Blake described and explained it in the Catalogue, recording the ancient legendary history out of whose fantastic imagery he had drawn so precisely the curious figures of his imagination. The picture was painted on canvas in what Blake called fresco and was about ten by fourteen feet.

In the last Battle of King Arthur, only Three Britons escaped; these were the Strongest Man, the Beautifullest Man, and the Ugliest Man; these three marched through the field unsubdued, as Gods, and the Sun of Britain set, but shall arise again with tenfold splendor when Arthur shall awake from sleep, and resume his dominion over earth and ocean.

If this picture was half as strange and as excellent as Blake believed it to be, it is a great pity that it has been lost to the world, like many another masterpiece. Frescoes on walls last as long as the walls they are painted on, but frescoes on unmounted canvas quickly crack and easily fall apart. All that has survived of "The Ancient Britons" is Blake's description and fragmentary comments by several of those fortunate ones who saw the exhibition and marveled at the picture.

For economy's sake the exhibition was held on the first floor of the hosiery shop of Blake's brother James. The chief attraction was the fresco of the Canterbury pilgrims. In addition there were sixteen "Poetical and Historical Inventions," eleven frescoes or water colors, and seven drawings.

As far as advertising was concerned, the exhibition was practically a secret.

The exhibition lasted from May until September 1809. There was no visitor's book to show who came. To the fashionable world of London, Blake's name was now largely unknown. His artist friends made no effort to persuade people of influence to attend, for painters seldom urge their patrons to go to other artists' exhibitions. But there was one inquiring visitor who recorded his impressions. He was Mr. Henry Crabb Robinson, a man who made it his business to know the interesting and important people of his time. His gossipy journal is a portrait gallery of the noted people he met.

Some rumor of Blake as an odd character had come to Robinson's ears, and his instinct for the unusual had led him to the unheralded display. Blake's brother James, who was in charge, ushered him into the empty rooms and handed him a copy of the Catalogue. Mr. Robinson glanced at the paintings with distaste and opened the Catalogue. Amazed at its extraordinary style and contents, he purchased four copies at half a crown each—which he thought quite an outlay—from the astonished James. As he left he asked, "Does this admit me again—er—free?"

"Oh! Free as long as you live," replied the delighted James.

Robinson gave a copy of A *Descriptive Catalogue* to his friend Charles Lamb, the brilliant essayist who spent his days in drudgery as a clerk at the East India House and his nights among the best minds in London. Lamb, attracted by Robinson's kindly wit and vivacity, often came to the latter's "evenings."

Lamb knew something of madness and tragedy, for his sister Mary had, during a fit of the insanity which recurred throughout her life, murdered her mother. Lamb devoted himself to caring tenderly for Mary, who possessed a brilliant mind and when free of her malady had collaborated with him in writing their famous *Tales from Shakespeare*.

The Catalogue and the pictures made so vivid an impression on Lamb that fifteen years later he recalled this experience in a letter to a friend, dated May 15, 1824.

. . . Blake is a real name, I assure you and a most extraordinary man, if he be still living. He is the Robert [William] Blake, whose wild designs accompany a splendid folio edition of the "Night Thoughts," which you may have seen. . . . He paints in water colours marvellous strange pictures, visions of his brain, which he asserts that he has seen. They have great merit. He has *seen* the old Welsh bards on Snowdon—he has seen the Beautifullest, the strongest, and the Ugliest Man, left alone from the Massacre of the Britons by the Romans, and has painted them from memory (I have seen his paint-

ings), and asserts them to be as good as the figures of Raphael and Angelo, but not better, as they had precisely the same retro-visions and prophetic visions with themself [himself].
. . . His Pictures—one in particular, the Canterbury Pilgrims (far above Stothard's)—have great merit, but hard, dry, yet with grace. He has written a Catalogue of them with a most spirited criticism on Chaucer, but mystical and full of Vision.
. . . the man is flown, whither I know not—to Hades or a Mad House. But I must look on him as one of the most extraordinary persons of the age. . . .

The exhibition was over. It was a complete failure. Except for a few catalogues, there had been no sales. Blake was deeply discouraged; Catherine and he together read from their Bible and took courage from its deep consolation. His angels in eternity seemed very far away, and he could not hear them saying, "There will be many exhibitions in great cities of the world, and trumpets of glory sounding your name, and, a hundred years from today, the lords of the earth will bid fortunes for a single little volume or sketch."

Late one night by the guttering candle he had written in his notebook:

Tuesday, January 20, 1807. Between Two and Seven in the Evening, Despair!

CHAPTER XXI

The Adventure of the Visionary Heads

. . . the Flea told him that all fleas were inhabited by the souls of such men as were by nature blood-thirsty to excess, and were therefore providentially confined to the size and form of insects; otherwise, were he himself, for instance, the size of a horse, he would depopulate a great portion of the country.
—John Varley: *A Treatise on Zodiacal Physiognomy*

Among the "enthusiasts" who admired Blake was John Varley, twenty years Blake's junior. Varley was an excellent water-color painter and a professional astrologer whose dismal prognostications came true so often that one man stayed in bed all day on the date Varley and the stars had set for his demise. On the same evening, sure that he had beaten fate, he arose, tripped over a coal scuttle, and fell downstairs into eternity.

Varley was delighted with Blake's visions and especially with Blake's statements that he actually saw the people he spoke with. Varley did not doubt this for one moment, and one evening he asked Blake to draw a portrait of one of his invisible guests. Blake took paper and pencil and began a drawing, for he did not like to disappoint the eager Mr. Varley.

As the evening wore on, Varley urged Blake to call up William Wallace to sit for his portrait. Blake peered keenly into space and made a careful drawing of a robust head with a very noble expression. Varley was greatly impressed, and called for Edward the First. He watched Blake, then scanned the blank wall where the lion of England was sitting for his portrait. Blake's portrait showed a mournful-looking hero with a somewhat reluctant expression. Upon request, Moses, Julius Caesar, and Watt Tyler posed in rapid succession.

But it was growing late; the spirits refused to pose for long sittings, and by two a.m. Blake quit. However, on other evenings lovely lady spirits sat for their portraits. While the beautiful Corinna, the Theban poetess, was sitting, with a particularly soulful expression on her face, who should flounce in but Lais, the courtesan. She rudely persisted in standing between Blake and the lovely Corinna until the latter's portrait was sketched. Blake said he had to sketch her in order to get rid of her, but he gave her likeness a particularly low and mean look.

Mr. Varley made notes on all the sketches. Sometimes Blake would stop and say, "I can't go on—it is gone," or, "It has moved; the mouth is gone," or, "He frowns; he is displeased with my portrait of him." Soon Varley had a portrait gallery drawn from the specters of some of the most respectable and a few of the most disreputable ghosts in history. Among them appeared "The Man Who Built the Pyramids," "King Saul," "Bathsheba," and "David," as well as a "Portrait of the Man who instructed Mr. Blake in Painting in his Dreams," and one inscribed, *"Richard Coeur de Lion drawn from his spectre. W. Blake fecit, Oct. 14, 1819, at quarter past twelve midnight."* The visionary heads are sketches full of the Blake vitality and imagination.

For the most part Blake had no interest in mediums,

spiritualists, and star-gazers who saw only with their mortal eyes. These he looked on as vulgar and unimaginative. He did paint one remarkable demon for Varley which he called "The Ghost of a Flea." All this created a great deal of fanciful rumor in London about Mr. Blake.

If Blake was pulling Varley's leg, as he sometimes did with superstitious "blockheads," he never smiled but solemnly acted out the pantomime of a portrait painter with an actual sitter. This would not be difficult for him, as he seldom used models, believing that they spoiled spiritual vision.

Any illustrator with a little imagination can draw imaginary heads, for this is a faculty by which he earns a living. Blake's burlesque may have deceived Varley, but it did his reputation as a serious artist no good, for it seemed to confirm those rumors of his madness which have even up to the present continued to damage his reputation, and he became known more widely as the man who had painted the ghost of a flea than as a great artist or poet.

When an old Baptist minister who had known Blake was asked if he did not think Blake was cracked, he replied, "Yes, but it is a crack that lets in the light."

CHAPTER XXII

Doctor Thornton

> . . . And I know that this World Is a World of Imagina-
> tion & Vision. I see Every thing I paint In This World,
> but Every body does not see alike. . . . The tree which
> moves some to tears of joy is in the Eyes of others only a
> Green thing which stands in the way. . . .

Dr. Robert John Thornton was a well-known physician and botanist. In addition to his successful practice, he found time to write books on the more picturesque aspects of botany, which he published in the most beautiful and costly formats possible, and at his own expense.

The Temple of Flora or Garden of the Poet, Painter, and Philosopher, like his other books, had not been a best-seller, and the heavy cost of publication had considerably impoverished its author. With undampened enthusiasm, the doctor proceeded to issue an edition of the Latin poet Virgil's *Pastorals* for use in schools. Happily, this work had met with considerable success and had gone into two editions.

Thornton now planned a third edition, which was to be especially attractive to the young because of its two hundred and forty illustrations in woodcut. This was probably the most over-illustrated edition of this classic ever printed.

A number of engravers were engaged for this work, and among them was Blake. Blake made twenty exquisite drawings in sepia which caught the lyric mood of the text.

Seventeen of these he engraved on wood, though he had never used this medium before. As usual he invented his own original technique that gave a rich and sparkling vitality to the page. His artist friends were delighted with this new and fresh approach to book illustration.

But when the drawings were submitted to the publishers they were rejected as rough and amateurish, and the hack engravers hooted in derision at what they considered their crudities. Doctor Thornton thought so himself; but, nonetheless, he took them to some of his distinguished artist friends. As he listened to the chorus of glowing praise he changed his mind, and the woodcuts were printed in the book, although they were ruthlessly cut down to fit the page, thus mutilating the long horizontal beauty of Blake's compositions.

These designs brought a fresh and vigorous influence into the dead and stuffy atmosphere of conventional book illustration. The luminosity and freedom of their technique, and their romantic mood, gave to the art of wood-engraving in England new possibilities for expression.

Doctor Thornton had a very narrow escape from oblivion, for he probably would have been completely forgotten if it had not been for the seventeen little woodcuts he had almost rejected.

One morning Mr. Fuseli, who was teacher at the Royal Academy's antique class, on entering the school was amazed to find his old friend Blake sitting before the life-size plaster cast of the *Laocoön*, absorbed in making a careful drawing of it.

"What! You here, Mr. Blake? We ought to come and learn of you, not you of us!"

Blake was pleased with the compliment and delighted to see his old friend. He enjoyed being among the students again, here where he had studied for a short time in his youth; and he amazed and confounded the disciples of Sir Joshua Reynolds by his startling precepts, so contrary to the sacred *Discourses* of their illustrious idol.

The drawing he was making was a study for an engraving, a commission for an illustration to a dull encyclopedia. The *Laocoön* was a complicated sculptural group of writhing snakes and figures which had been admired by Michelangelo and was mistakenly considered one of the masterpieces of Greek art.

Afterward Blake inscribed on the limbs of the figures in the engraving sayings from the curious wisdom in which his mind was steeped—such as:

Prayer is the Study of Art.
Praise is the Practice of Art.
The Whole Business of Man is Art.
You must leave Fathers & Mothers & Houses & Lands if they stand in the way of Art.
Art can never exist without Naked Beauty displayed.
A Poet, a Painter, a Musician, an Architect: the Man or Woman who is not one of these is not a Christian.

For a few moments the tedium of the classroom had been electrified and illumined by Blake's presence. As the door closed after the venerable visitor, dullness again settled on the classic labors of Mr. Fuseli's students.

"Don't mind him," piped the youngest student. "He's only the madman who painted the ghost of a flea."

"Madman—perhaps," said Fuseli severely as he sketched an anatomical diagram of the forearm on the drawing before him. "Madman—and genius—who will be remembered long, long after all of us are forgotten." He smiled wistfully, remembering something he had said long ago, "He's a good man to steal from!" But he said nothing more.

PART FIVE

Fountain Court

(1821-1827)

. . . I have travel'd thro' Perils & Darkness not unlike a
Champion. I have Conquer'd, and shall Go on Conquering.

CHAPTER XXIII

The Book of Job

(1821-1823)

. . . Why is the Bible more Entertaining & Instructive than any other book? Is it not because they are addressed to the Imagination, which is Spiritual Sensation, & but mediately to the Understanding or Reason?

In 1821 the Blakes moved from South Molton Street to a first-floor apartment of two rooms at Number 3 Fountain Court, a house occupied by his brother-in-law. This was a respectable brick residence on a quiet courtyard just off the Strand. From the rear window between brick walls they could catch a glimpse of the Thames. The yellow gleam of light on water and the blue haze of open country beyond was a familiar vista that Blake had loved since boyhood.

They arranged living quarters in the back room, where there was space enough for him to work. The front room was used as a reception room and a gallery for the display of his work. Catherine kept things neat and tidy, though the furniture was worn and shabby. Near his worktable he hung a print of Dürer's "Melancholia."

The Blakes had always been able to manage the economy of living and William had never been in debt, but the move to Fountain Court had involved extra expenses, and there were no reserve funds to meet them. For a young beginner this would have been difficult enough, but for a man in his sixties it was a desperate dilemma. The only thing he could turn into cash was his collection of prints, a treasure he had been collecting for a lifetime. Sadly he gathered them together (all except the "Melancholia") and took them to Colnaghi, who was glad to buy them for a fair price.

Many of his old friends had gone, and, of those who remained, few called on him. Among these was George Cumberland, who had in 1818 introduced to Blake twenty-six-year-old John Linnell, the portrait painter. The young man was immediately delighted with Blake's art and brought his artist friends of the new generation to admire the neglected master. When Linnell heard of Blake's financial difficulty he took the story to Sir Thomas Lawrence and other well-to-do artists who were members of the Royal Academy. The result was that the council of the Royal Academy voted a donation of twenty-five pounds, which Linnell presented to Blake.

John Linnell was not wealthy—portrait painting was a precarious means of earning a living—but his admiration and affection for the aging Blake were such that he made genuine sacrifices to see that the artist and his wife were not in want and that Blake was able to work free from worry about the immediate necessities of life.

When he saw a set of twenty-one water colors for *The Book of Job* that Blake had made for Thomas Butts, Linnell gave him the order for a duplicate set and proposed that he make a series of engravings from them. Blake was enthusiastic. A business arrangement was drawn up by which Blake was to receive a hundred pounds for the finished plates and a hundred pounds out of the profits, if any. Linnell was to own the plates and copyright and to furnish the copperplates. Although there were no profits, Linnell paid Blake fifty pounds in installments as the work progressed during 1825 and 1826.

A dutiful son could not have watched over or more lovingly provided for an aging father than the young portrait painter cared for the grand old poet-prophet who was laboriously fashioning the most superb vision of his long career.

On his frequent visits Linnell saw the designs of Job's epic drama emerging on the little copperplates. Steadily, for weeks and months, Blake's strong wrist traced the outlines and modeling, line by line. From time to time he inked and printed the unfinished plates to see what he had done so far. These proofs were called first, second, third "states" —and so on—and showed how far he had progressed with the engraving.

Blake had conceived his theme as a universal allegory of life itself. It was a spiritual autobiography as well, for the figures of the venerable Job with flowing mane, and his faithful wife ever beside him, typified William and Catherine Blake in their journey through life.

As the plates progressed, he added decorative borders with lettered inscriptions from the Bible. Lastly, he engraved a twenty-second plate with a title-page design. This work took the best part of three years. The first printing of the book was in three editions, priced as follows: ordinary edition, 3 guineas; proof edition, 5 guineas; India paper edition, 6 guineas.

Linnell, though he was not a businessman, undertook

the sale of the book through his personal efforts. There
were no advance notices or advertising of any kind. It received no reviews. A few friends bought copies.

After a century, *The Book of Job* has become Blake's
most famous and best-known work. Of all the designs in the
book, "When the morning Stars sang together & all the
Sons of God shouted for Joy" is the one most often associ-
ated with his name.

Blake, unperturbed by the fate of *The Book of Job* in the
unseeing eyes of mortals, turned to the completion of his
painting of "The Last Judgment."

While he was working on the plates for *Job*, Linnell had
proposed that Blake should design and engrave a set of
illustrations for Dante. Not satisfied with the English trans-
lations, Blake studied Italian, in a few weeks mastering
enough of the language to read *The Divine Comedy* in
Italian. Languages had always fascinated him, and he had
studied Latin, Greek, Hebrew, and French.

On a visit to Fountain Court, Linnell found his friend
laid up in bed with a sprained ankle. "I have brought you a
present," he said, and handed Blake a sketchbook of beautiful Dutch paper in folio size. "It is for you and for Dante,"
he said with a smile.

As Blake lovingly turned the blank pages, designs began
to appear on their glowing whiteness. Catherine and Linnell
propped him up in bed till he was comfortable, and gave
him his pencils. When he had filled the book, there were
one hundred and two drawings. Some were only a few magic
lines indicating a motif; others were elaborate designs rich
in ornament and detail. Linnell provided seven large cop-

perplates, and on these Blake began engraving his drawings.
The Dante was a heroic task and was never finished. But
the drawings remain as one of the most beautiful series
of his designs.

At Fountain Court there was an atmosphere of peace and
spiritual harmony—an aura of beauty that permeated the
quiet sanctuary where the Blakes lived and worked. Old
friends and new acquaintances alike felt their presence like
a benediction when they came to call upon the patriarchal
poet-painter and his wife. The obscure courtyard off the
teeming highway of the city was a symbol. Worldly fame
and material fortune had passed Blake by, and he now lived
humbly and content. Often it seemed that he and Catherine were on the verge of poverty and want, but each day
met its needs. He printed copies of the Prophetic Books
and songs to fill infrequent orders. His teeming brain was
never idle. The old creative fires of inspiration still burned,
but with an even richer, mellower glow.

Since his childhood he had loved the poetry of Spenser,
Milton, and Shakespeare. Of these Milton was his favorite
for grandeur, and Blake had made him the hero of one of his
Prophetic Books. He had made a set of designs for *Paradise
Lost* and later a group of twelve for *Paradise Regained*, and
there had been twelve more for *L'Allegro* and *Il Penseroso*.
For Milton's *Comus* he had painted a series of fantasies
steeped in the magic of that haunted revel. Each design was
a unique invention, with a plastic life all its own.

A hundred years before Blake's time John Bunyan had
written *Pilgrim's Progress*—while spending twelve years in
jail for talking too much. This Puritan novel of the soul's

adventures on the perilous journey to salvation had fascinated Blake, and he painted twenty-two exquisite water
colors for it.

He and Catherine no longer took the long walks in the
country. He went out only to walk across the court to the
Coalhole Tavern for his daily pint of porter. Londoners did
not drink water, as it was considered unhealthy (not without reason), and its scarcity made bathing an infrequent
practice. Water was had from the public pumps in the
nearest square or from the street vender who sold "pure
river water" from door to door. The city had no drainage
system, and the gutters in the middle of the streets ran
foul with slops poured from window or doorway.

Blake received occasional visits from Crabb Robinson,
the same man who in days gone by had visited his one-man
exhibition and had bought four copies of *A Descriptive
Catalogue*. Robinson's visits were in the nature of a re-
porter's interview, an exchange of questions and answers in
which Robinson shrewdly tried to probe the mystery of
Blake's mind. These interviews he recorded in his journal
and so left a vivid portrait of Blake and a record of their
conversations for posterity.

Crabb Robinson was particularly inquisitive about the
spirit world. He read Wordsworth aloud to Blake, to his
great delight. Robinson bought a copy of *Songs of Innocence* and a picture. "Blake spoke of his horror of money
and of turning pale when it was offered him. And this was
certainly unfeigned."

"I have had," he said, "much intercourse with Voltaire,
and he said to me, 'I blasphemed the Son of Man, and it

shall be forgiven me, but they [the enemies of Voltaire] blasphemed the Holy Ghost in me, and it shall not be forgiven to them.' "

Mr. Crabb Robinson wanted more specific details. "I asked him in what language Voltaire spoke. His answer was ingenious and gave no encouragement to cross-questioning: 'To my sensations it was English. It was like the touch of a musical key: he touched it probably French, but to my ear it became English.' "

Robinson told Blake of the death of his old friend Flaxman, the sculptor, and Blake said with a smile, "I thought I should have gone first."

In his notebook Blake scribbled a wry tribute to his old friend Fuseli:

> The only Man that e'er I knew
> Who did not make me almost spew
> Was Fuseli: he was both Turk & Jew—
> And so, dear Christian Friends, how do you do?

This was the old manuscript notebook that he had kept for years. It still held the first draft of "Tyger! Tyger!" and the final verses, his *Public Address*, and *A Vision of the Last Judgment*.

CHAPTER XXIV

A Vision of the Last Judgment

Whenever any Individual Rejects Error and Embraces Truth, a Last Judgment has been passed on that Individual.

Blake stepped away from his work, tilting back his head and peering through half-closed eyes at the large canvas on which he was painting, though the room was, even then, too small for him to get the full effect of his work as a whole.

The cool light from the north window fell on his massive head fringed with white hair, and on his broad shoulders, unbowed under the weight of his sixty-seven years. Sketches and studies for the painting cluttered the walls of the room, and on the long worktable beside him lay his notebook among the bright little pans of water color. In the farther corner stood the heavy etching press, and on shelves above were rows of copperplates and the paraphernalia of the engraver's art.

Occupying the center of the room stood the nearly completed painting of "The Last Judgment." The canvas was perhaps seven by five feet, though the hundreds of figures that filled its surface seemed to extend outward into infinite space. Tiers of them extended from top to bottom, culminating in a vision of Christ seated on the Throne of Judgment, surrounded by four trumpeting angels. On His right hand the just ascended, exulting in swirling spirals; and on his left the writhing damned plunged head downward into the flaming pit. In the center a column of characters from the Bible rose in a majestic allegory. A thousand figures moving in rhythmic flow invested the canvas with an awesome grandeur. Over its surface, films of color flickered in bright sequences that in places glowed like gold and silver.

From time to time he paused and wrote in the notebook that lay on the table his thoughts on the theme he was painting.

The Last Judgment is an Overwhelming of Bad Art & Science. Mental Things are alone Real; what is call'd Corporeal, Nobody Knows of its Dwelling Place: it is in Fallacy, & its Existence an Imposture. Where is the Existence out of Mind or Thought? Where is it but in the Mind of a Fool? Some People flatter themselves that there will be No Last Judgment & that Bad Art will be adopted & mixed with Good Art, That Error or Experiment will make a Part of Truth, & they Boast that it is its Foundation; these People flatter themselves: I will not Flatter them. . . . Truth is Eternal. Error, or Creation, will be Burned up, & then, & not till Then, Truth, or Eternity will appear. It is Burnt up the Moment Men cease to behold it.

The Last Judgment was a subject that had delighted the masters of the past from earliest times, and the painters of the Renaissance had resolved it into a melodrama so florid and terrifying that it had sent shudders through the souls of sinners for centuries—without, however, noticeably improving human behavior.

The theme of the picture had been in Blake's mind for many years. In 1807 he had used it for a drawing for Blair's

The Grave. At that time his friend Cumberland, the miniature painter, had shown it to Mr. Hayley's friend the Countess of Egremont. When the Countess went into raptures over it, Cumberland persuaded her to commission Blake to make a water color of it. Blake had through the years developed and enriched the theme, and now it was taking shape as the intricate composition on the large canvas which he was completing.

He had written innumerable manuscripts, poems, and plays—more than Shakespeare's and Milton's work put together, he claimed. They had all been rejected by the publishers. When a manuscript was returned he said, "Well, it will be published elsewhere," and added with a mysterious smile, "and beautifully bound."

Writing and painting were his recreation from the exacting labor of engraving. When a friend asked if he never wanted a holiday, he replied, "I don't understand what you mean by wanting a holiday!" Expression and creative work were holiday and ecstasy, even when he was ill. A young friend once complained that he was too ill to work; what should he do? "What to do!" was the reply. "Why, I work on whether ill or not. I never stop for anything."

But for all artists and writers there come periods when the ideas cease to flow and when the inspiration no longer pours. There are dark voids when the days go by and there is no light. One afternoon a forlorn young disciple dropped in to tea. He had not been able to work for two weeks. "What does one do when there is no inspiration?"

Blake turned to Catherine and said cheerily, "Why! It's just so with us. And what do we do then, Kate?"

"We kneel down and pray, Mr. Blake," said Catherine

very positively. Mr. Blake laid a reassuring hand on the young artist's shoulder.

Once a month Blake's young painter friends gathered at 3 Fountain Court to listen to the new gospel of art from the lips of "the Interpreter" (as they called Blake). Each new invention of the old master they greeted with rapture, as a revelation of the new heaven and the new earth. He read to them his unpublished *Public Address*, which they hailed as a manifesto of a new movement, applauding its fervor and indignation.

No Man of Sense ever supposes that copying from Nature is the Art of Painting; if Art is no more than this, it is no better than any other Manual Labour; anybody may do it & the fool often will do it best as it is a work of no Mind. . . .

"I know my Execution is not like Any Body Else. I do not intend it should be so; none but Blockheads Copy one another. My Conception & Invention are on all hands allow'd to be Superior. My Execution will be found so too. To what is it that Gentlemen of the first Rank both in Genius & Fortune have subscribed their Names? To my Inventions. . . .

The young men who listened so avidly to him were going to be the disciples of this new doctrine in art. They were very young and the world was very green. If it was dull and stupid and academic, they would change all that. They would make it over, with vision and imagination. They were a dedicated band, a brotherhood of the new movement. Perversely they called themselves "The Ancients."

The watchword of the Ancients was Poetry and Sentiment. They loved to go on sketching tramps, startling the villagers with their strange costumes and their camp stools (then a new invention). They affected amazing cloaks, went unshorn and turned day and night topsy-turvy. They recited Virgil under trees, improvised tragedies in the haunted Black Lane, and were given to singing Locke's Macbeth music at night in hollow clefts and deserted chalk pits. They sat up for sunrises, they rushed out into the worst thunderstorms. They made friends with the village idiots and ostlers. They experimented in new techniques; and a forgotten bottle of egg mixture once exploded horribly in a pocket during a visit to London. They courted ridicule and affronted fashion, since they despised worldly success as much as worldly scorn. Yet lazily and intermittently as they labored, their pictures became intense with a peculiar beauty of their own.*

This happy frenzy was not the mantle of Elijah or of Blake. These youngsters were not fashioned as was their master, out of the iron and steel that can pass through the fiery ordeal of genius. In fact, as the disciples grew middle-aged and respectable, they renounced Blake and became critical of his rebellious philosophy. His friend Samuel Palmer suggested that his works, if not expurgated, would "be excluded from every drawing-room table in England." After Blake's death his manuscript notebook was sold for ten shillings to the poet-painter Dante Gabriel Rossetti, who shared its treasures with the poet Algernon Swinburne. These two recognized the qualities of the forgotten genius and worked to restore his fame. The treasured notebook was to become celebrated as the "Rossetti Manuscript."

* *William Blake: His Philosophy and Symbols,* by Samuel Foster Damon. London: Constable and Co. Ltd., 1924.

CHAPTER XXV

Sunflower Weary of Time

Ah, Sun-flower! weary of time,
Who countest the steps of the Sun,
Seeking after that sweet golden clime
Where the traveller's journey is done.

On Sunday mornings Blake would put on his old-fashioned black suit and broad-brimmed hat and pay his weekly visit to the Linnell family at the Collins farm, North End, Hampstead. Linnell had rented part of an old farmhouse in an attractive rural setting and moved there with his family, keeping the studio where he worked in London.

Though it was possible to go there by coach, Blake preferred to walk over the Heath, starting in the morning and returning after dark. He sometimes stopped on the way there to pick up his young friend Samuel Palmer, one of the "Ancients" who painted landscapes with a fine personal vision.

As he came over the hill and sighted the Collins farm the Linnell children would run out, shouting, to meet him, for he had made them his special friends and confidants, with his marvelous stories and the drawings he sometimes brought along. There was one of a grasshopper which was their particular favorite. As he watched them at play he would smile and say, "That is heaven." Stroking the head

Carnegie Public Library
Robinson, Illinois

of a little girl, he said, "May God make this world as beautiful to you, my child, as it has been to me."

The children, the farm animals, the quiet garden, and the rural scene filled him with utter content. It was good to sit and talk through the long afternoon with Varley, Linnell, and Dr. Thornton about visionary art and the power of the imagination, each one offering his own interpretation of the invisible universe and its peculiar inhabitant, Man.

In the evenings he listened with brimming eyes to Mrs. Linnell singing Scottish songs. Sometimes he himself would sing his songs to music of his own composition.

Then, with Mrs. Linnell's shawl about his shoulder and a family servant carrying a lantern, he would return across the Heath under the stars to Catherine and Fountain Court.

But more and more Blake was becoming confined by ill health, and his visits to Linnell at Hampstead Heath were less frequent.

There were attacks of illness when he was in bed for several days, with intense pain. But he worked on persistently, sick or well. He was lavishing all he knew on his great fresco painting of "The Last Judgment." The engravings for *Job* were completed. The hundred and two drawings for *The Divine Comedy* were sketched in, and the seven engraved plates progressed line by line.

Linnell introduced his friend the famous portrait painter Sir Thomas Lawrence to Blake, who had so severely criticized his art in the past. The great man was delighted with Blake's work and bought a copy of the *Songs of Innocence* and two water colors, "Queen Catherine's Dream" and "The Wise and Foolish Virgins." This picture he said was his favorite, and he kept it on a table where he could always see it.

Frederick Tatham, one of Blake's young disciples, ordered an illuminated print of "The Ancient of Days." It was one of Blake's favorite subjects, one which he loved to color. He put the last bright touches on the streaming hair, held it triumphantly at arm's length for a moment, then tossed it aside, saying, "There, that will do! I cannot mend it."

The strength of his body was waning, but his thinking was still vital and clear. "I am going to a land I have long wished to see," he said; and looking at Catherine sitting by his bedside, he said suddenly, "Keep just as you are! You have been ever an angel to me: I will draw you."

It was Sunday, August 12, 1827. As the late-afternoon light waned he began to sing as one inspired. The words and music came from another world. They were the songs of "A bird that was born for joy." As Catherine leaned over him he said, "My beloved, they are not mine—no, they are not mine. We will not be parted. I will always be about you to take care of you."

His countenance became serene, and a deep peace settled upon him, and he burst into singing of the things he saw in heaven.

"In truth it was the death of a saint," someone standing by him observed. Catherine recalled wistfully, "Mr. Blake has been so little with me. For though in the body we were never separated, he was incessantly away in Paradise."

CHAPTER XXVI

"*Not Unlike a Champion*"

Reengraved time after time
Ever in their youthful prime
My designs unchanged remain
Time may rage but rage in vain
For above time's troubled fountains
On the great Atlantic mountains
In my golden house on high
There they shine eternally.

Catherine gathered up the prints and drawings into port-folios. There were the copperplates of the Prophetic Books, of *Job* and many others, and a great store of unpublished manuscripts, as well as the notebook. Of worldly goods or material estate he left nothing—only a treasure of beauty and of joy for a thousand generations, a legacy of genius that could never be measured. If this legacy could be put on sale today, eager buyers would offer millions.

He was buried in an unmarked grave by a few friends. Tatham came a distance of ninety miles to attend the funeral. But although Blake had known and been admired by some of the distinguished people of his time, he was soon strangely and completely forgotten, though his influence was carried on in the painting of a few of his disciples. Linnell and Tatham cared for Catherine for the four remaining years before she joined Blake. She left to Tatham the treasure of Blake's unpublished works, and over a period of forty years he sold them, from time to time, to unknown buyers. Like many others, he had doubts about the ideas expressed in Blake's writings. When he joined a religious sect called "the Irvingites" he decided that Blake's doctrines were false and that his writings should be destroyed: it is said he spent two days burning some hundred of Blake's manuscripts! Fortunately the two great collections of Blake's paintings belonging to Butts and Linnell remained intact, and Linnell kept the manuscript notebook.

The two large paintings of "The Ancient Britons" and "The Last Judgment" have utterly and mysteriously disappeared. The moist English climate and damp storage may account for this. Aside from Blake's elaborate description, the only record of their existence is in the memory of a few fortunate persons who claimed to have seen them many years before.

The Linnell and the Butts collections of Blake's pictures were auctioned at Christie's in London, and are now occasionally publicly exhibited in the great museums and libraries of England and America. The plates of the *Job* were given to the British Museum.

Many admirable and instructive books have been written by learned men on the meaning and symbolism of Blake's poetry and pictures. Sometimes these works seem more mysterious and incomprehensible to the ordinary person than Blake's works themselves. But the not-too-ordinary person—and especially "Children, who have taken a greater delight in contemplating my Pictures than I even hoped" —can enjoy the lyric beauty and tender music of Blake's poems and pictures in a very direct and enriching way by simply reading and looking at them. If you look long enough and listen often enough they explain themselves. They say, "I am Vision and Delight. I am Exuberance and Joy!"

Long before his death he had written to Thomas Butts:

And now let me finish with assuring you that, Tho' I have been very unhappy, I am so no longer. I am again Emerged into the light of day; I still & shall to Eternity Embrace Christianity and Adore him who is the Express image of God; but I have travel'd thro' Perils & Darkness not unlike a Champion. I have Conquer'd, and shall go on Conquering. Nothing can withstand the fury of my Course among the Stars of God & in the Abysses of the Accuser. My enthusiasm is still what it was, only enlarged and confirmed.

Notes on Blake's Designs
for the Book of Job

Notes on Blake's Designs
for the Book of Job

The Book of Job is a profound epic poem containing some of the most beautiful language ever written. Blake, by his genius for depicting abstract ideas in concrete visual forms, created a series of dramatic pictures that tell the story of Job as seen through his own intense personal vision. They are (like the poem) really a play. The theme is the struggle between good and evil and the search for man's identity taking place in his own consciousness. Besides endowing them richly with meanings and allusions, Blake has organized his designs in powerful rhythms of line and form that create a flow of movement, a thrust and counterthrust that are balanced within the picture frame. It is largely by means of these "inventions" that he is able to give such startling vitality to his "visions." Few artists have ever attained the intensity of feeling through visual communication with which Blake supercharges so many of his pictures.

All great paintings are mysterious. They never reveal their secret, and so we come back to them again and again to discover in them new depths of meaning and delight. Their challenge awakens the greatness within us. This may suggest rather than explain the timeless fascination and eternal freshness of Blake's pictures for the Book of Job.

I

Thus did Job continually.

This is the Job family.

Job, and his wife, their three daughters, and their seven shepherd sons are gathered under the tree of life. Job's wife is not mentioned in the Bible but Blake has made her Job's inseparable companion.

All are dutifully at prayer, a picture of untried innocence and virtue. The sheep in the foreground are sound asleep. Even the shepherd dog dozes comfortably with a lamb for a pillow. Intellect is asleep. Musical instruments (the arts) hang neglected on the tree. The Jobs are too materially comfortable to be interested in the arts. In the background on their right (the spiritual side) the sun is setting behind the church. On their left (the material side) the moon is rising. There is one bright star.

In all the designs the right (of the actors) signifies the spiritual and the left the material.

Blake made twenty-one water colors for the Book of Job on commission from his patron Thomas Butts in 1821. These are now owned by the Fogg Art Museum of Harvard University. Plates I, III, IV, V, VI, IX, XVI, XVII, XVIII, XIX, XX are here reproduced from this set through the courtesy of the Fogg Art Museum.

In 1823 Blake's devoted admirer John Linnell commissioned him to paint and engrave replicas of the Butts set. Plates II, VII, VIII, X, XI, XII, XIII, XIV, XV, XXI from the Linnell set are reproduced with the kind permission of the Pierpont Morgan Library (New York).

II

When the Almighty was yet with me, when my children were about me.

The scene is pictured on three levels. Above, the Almighty sits enthroned with the Book of the Word open before him. He is surrounded by celestial beings. Beneath the throne Satan suddenly appears, all fire and energy, asking that he may test Job's faith.

Below, on the material plane, the Job family sit unperturbed. On their right the two angels called in the Bible "My two witnesses" float, barely touching the earth.

III

Thy sons and thy daughters were eating and drinking wine in their eldest brother's house: and, behold, there came a great wind from the wilderness and smote upon the four faces of the house, and it fell upon the young men, and they are dead.

At the feast of Job's children Satan visits fire and destruction upon them. None escape save one messenger who brings the news of disaster to Job. The design is a pyramid of intricately woven forms. Satan with bat wings crouches exultantly above the falling walls, flame pouring from his outstretched hands. Job is suddenly to be confronted with the age-old question, "Does God permit senseless disaster to overtake his innocent creatures?"

IV

I only am escaped alone to tell thee.

A messenger arrives, bringing the dreadful news to Job and his wife. Job lifts his eyes in anguish but his faith in God remains unshaken. The furious thrusting motion of the figure rushing in on the reader's left is countered in the design and its balance maintained by the S-shaped mass of the two figures and sheep on the right.

Carnegie Public Library
Robinson, Illinois

V

So, Satan went forth from the presence of the Lord.

Above, God closes the Book. The celestial chorus turns away in horror from the scene beneath. A flaming Satan plunges from the foot of the throne emptying the vial of his wrath on the innocent head of Job, who is performing an act of human kindness. On either side hover the two witnesses. This presents Job with another difficult question. Does God punish man for doing good?

VI

And smote Job with sore boils from the sole of his foot to the crown of his head.

Satan stands exultant on the prostrate body of Job. From his outstretched arms the flames and arrows of affliction pour down on his anguished victim. Job's feet are supported on the knees of his sorrowing wife, who covers her face in grief.

In the background, dark clouds fill the sky and the sun sinks in the sea of error. Although in anguish and despair, Job still holds his face heavenward. Though evil seems triumphant, Job remains firm in his faith. The powerful design is based on a triangular structure.

VII

And when they lifted up their eyes afar off, and knew him
not, they lifted up their voice, and wept.

Job's three friends have heard the bad news and are come
to magnify misery with clamor and sympathy. They are taking his calamity even harder than Job. Job is no longer on his
back. He leans against his wife, who is supporting him on her
knees. In the background, ruins stand among the barren hills.
Behind them the sun has set. (The structure of this design is
similar to that in number iv.)

VIII

Let the day perish wherein I was born.

Complete dejection bows to the ground the three friends and even Job's wife. But not Job. He now is upright, his arms uplifted in protest and appeal to God. He does not accept the conventional arguments of his pious friends who urge him to repent of sins he has not committed.

Job knows he has not sinned, for God made man in the divine image. He wants to know why he must suffer. Is evil more powerful than good? Job wants to know and understand.

The sky is clouded and the landscape bleak.

This is another pyramid design with the usual right-left symbolism.

IX

Then a Spirit passed before my face.

This is one of Blake's most majestic visions. At the base of
the picture, on the material plane, Job and his wife and friends
sit gazing at a vision wherein Job sees himself awakening in
the night. The darkness is illumined, the clouds roll back, and
a shining figure appears clothed with the sun. What is this
mysterious image? It is not a person but a presence. Is it the
Absolute, the Infinite, Truth itself? After darkness and doubt
comes the moment of revelation; the divine image appears to
the seeker for Truth.

X

The just upright man is laughed to scorn.

The vision has vanished and Job is again on the material plane.

His friends are reproaching him with accusing fingers. Even his wife urges him to curse God and die. Why does he not acknowledge that God sent deserved punishment upon him for his sins? Why does he not admit them and repent? How dare he question or argue with God? ask his orthodox friends. Job remains convinced that he has not sinned. He will not believe that God punishes the innocent. He rejects their false accusations. His faith in God's goodness and love is unshaken. He kneels upright, with sorrowful face uplifted.

XI

Then thou scarest me with dreams and terrifiest me through visions.

Job is again prostrated by fears and doubts. Satan, known by his cloven hoof, appears in the likeness of God, pointing to the tables of the law. Evil claims to be almighty. Scaly demons, evil suggestions, try to chain and drag him down in the fires of mental anguish. Job turns his face away from the deceiver and with upraised hands utterly rejects evil's claim to almighty power.

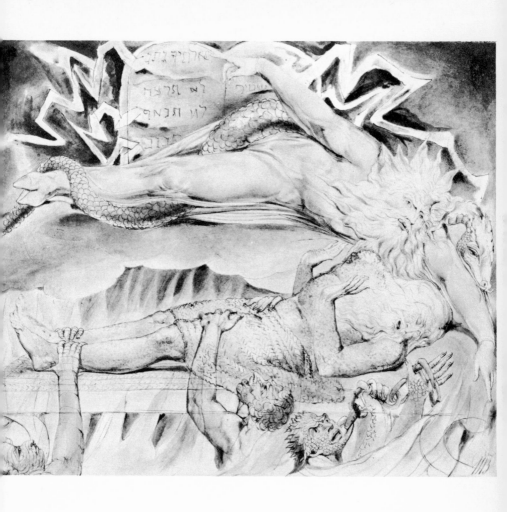

XII

I am young, and ye are very old; wherefore I was afraid.

Job has dispelled the obsessive illusion and finds himself again sitting with his wife and three friends. A young man appears on Job's right. He is called Elihu. Though very young he nevertheless demands to be heard. With superb gestures he eloquently reproaches both Job and his friends, but merely repeats the arguments of Job's accusers. Job's wife has become excessively bored and depressed by the situation. The friends are silent and Job listens glumly.

XIII

Then answered the Lord unto Job out of the whirlwind.

Job has retained his integrity. He has a vision of God as supreme good filling the universe. The accompanying whirlwind indicates the everpresence and almighty power of God, Truth. The three friends cannot see the divine glory with their material eyes and turn away and bow to the ground before Job and his wife.

XIV

When the morning stars sang together, and all the sons of
God shouted together for joy.

This is one of Blake's most perfect designs, and certainly
the most celebrated. Its exalted mood is one of the high
peaks in all Christian art.

Job, his wife, and his friends, enclosed in the cave of the
material senses, are gazing rapturously upward at the celestial
vision. Directly above them the heavenly Father kneels with
arms stretched wide. Beneath and behind are the Day and
his horses of energy (right) and Night driving the serpents of
darkness (left). Above, the sons of God with uplifted arms
and wings are shouting for joy. Blake had probably heard
Handel's great oratorio, "The Messiah." This design sounds
with the melodious thunder of the "Hallelujah" chorus.

Carnegie Public Library
Robinson, Illinois

XV

Behold now behemoth, which I made with thee.

This "invention" reads from the top down. God, flanked by the two witnesses, points with his left hand to the globe beneath. Job, his wife (right) and friends (left) gaze downward, spellbound. The circle of the earth is filled with the monstrous images of Behemoth (the land) and the dragon Leviathan (the sea).

Blake has endeavored to picture these strange creatures as described in the poem: "Behold now behemoth, which I made with thee: he eateth grass as an ox. . . . Canst thou draw out leviathan with an hook? or his tongue with a cord which thou lettest down?"

XVI

Hell is naked before him, and destruction hath no covering.

Evil is exposed and plunges to oblivion.

The ancient of days, the Almighty, sits enthroned in light with the Book again opened in his lap. The two witnesses ascend on either side on outspread wings.

Beneath, Satan the accuser and his two dark angels plunge head downward in flames into the burning pit of oblivion.

Below on the picture's right Job and his wife kneel beholding with upturned faces the awesome vision. On the left the false counselors cringe in terror.

XVII

I have heard of thee by the hearing of the ear:
but now mine eye seeth thee.

The sun of faith and understanding has rolled back the clouds of doubt, and the Eternal stands revealed in all-pervading light. With outstretched arms he blesses Job and his wife.

Kneeling before Him unafraid, they see God face to face.

On the left, the false counselors who had talked so much about God are turned away, for their material eyes cannot bear the brightness of His glory.

The design is a pronounced triangular organization with a powerful right-to-left movement (light dispelling darkness).

XVIII

The Lord also accepted Job.

In this design of Job's thanksgiving a pyramid pattern terminates in the point of flame reaching up into the sun. Job's outstretched arms, the arc of the clouds, and line of the hills give a powerful uplifting movement to the whole design. This picture is one of the rare moments in inspirational art.

XIX

Every man also gave him a piece of money.

The scene is again on the human plane.

Job and his wife are now at peace with the world, as is manifested in kindly human relations. In humility without humiliation they accept the gifts and kindnesses of their neighbors. The abundant grain is ripe for harvesting and the tree of life shelters them with its leaves of healing.

XX

And in all the land were no women found so fair as the daughters of Job: and their father gave them inheritance.

Job's three fair daughters listen dreamily as Job with out-stretched arms recounts his visions. The background is enriched with circles in which are suggested the episodes from Job's story. Here Blake interprets women's rights to be divine — a God-bestowed inheritance, as the Bible states.

XXI

*So the Lord blessed the latter end of Job more than
his beginning.*

Job has found his true spiritual identity and fulfillment in
his unity with God. He is again united with his family. They
are grouped as in the first design. They now stand upright
praising instead of praying. They all join in rejoicing. All are
singing and playing on the musical instruments that before
were idle. Even the sheep are waking up.

Blake has pictured not only his autobiography but the universal drama taking place in every human consciousness. Does
the timeless fascination of these majestic designs lie in the fact
that in some mysterious way we sense in them our own inner
experience — the hopes, struggles, and triumphs of the human
spirit?

Is it that you and I are Job?

Important Collections of Blake's Pictures, Prints, and Books in the United States

The Pierpont Morgan Library (New York). Water colors (including the Job set), prints, and the illuminated books. One of the most important collections. Shown by appointment or on request.

The Frick Collection (New York). The twenty-four exquisite water colors for John Bunyan's *Pilgrim's Progress*. This is a rare feast which should be seen by every Blake lover. Shown by appointment.

The Metropolitan Museum of Art (New York). Several important water colors and prints, including "The Wise and Foolish Virgins" and "Elisha in the Chariot of Fire." Shown on request.

The New York Public Library, Prints Division. Engraving of "Chaucer's Canterbury Pilgrims" and books illustrated with Blake's engravings. Also 1813 edition of Robert Blair's *The Grave*, with engravings designed by Blake, and a first edition of engravings for Edward Young's *Night Thoughts*. Shown on request.

Fogg Art Museum, Harvard University, Cambridge, Massachusetts. A superb set of the Job water colors, interesting to compare with those in the Pierpont Morgan Library. Shown on request.

The Boston Museum of Fine Arts. A large and important collection, including the Milton series. Other important water colors and prints. Shown on request.

The Huntington Library, San Marino, California. Hand-colored prints, pencil drawings, oil paintings, all the engraved work, most of the illuminated books. Water colors for the Nativity set and for Milton's *Paradise Lost* and *Comus*. The library's catalogue of Blake material, compiled by C. H. C. Baker, is worth having.

Alverthorpe Gallery, Jenkintown, Pennsylvania. The Lessing J. Rosenwald collection of Blake prints, drawings (including the "Visionary Heads"), and books illuminated by Blake is housed in the Alverthorpe Gallery and may be seen by appointment arranged in advance by writing to the Curator of Graphic Arts, National Gallery of Art, Washington, D.C.

NOTE: By far the best selection of Blake's prose and poetry easily and inexpensively available is contained in *The Portable Blake*, published by the Viking Press in both clothbound and paperbound editions. This volume includes *Songs of Innocence* and *Songs of Experi*ence complete, selections from other Blake works; notes about Blake from Crabb Robinson's *Reminiscences*; reproductions of twenty-one engravings from Blake's *Illustrations of the Book of Job*; and a chronology listing Blake's works and authoritative books about him.